Table of Contents

The Marian Miracle

Understanding Her Role

by

Dr. ant

Please remember that Internet websites listed in this work may have changed or disappeared between when this work was written and when it is read.

Contents

Introduction

When we gaze upon the tapestry of the Christian faith, we see shimmering threads woven with unparalleled beauty and grace. Among these, none shine more brilliantly than the life and virtues of the Blessed Virgin Mary. To the eyes of the believer, Mary stands like an ethereal beacon guiding us through the tumultuous seas of life to the serene shores of divine communion. She is not merely a figure painted in the sacred pages of Scripture, nor is she confined to the lofty heights of theological discourse; Mary is a living, breathing presence whose influence permeates every aspect of our spiritual journey.

Mary, the Mother of God, envelops us in a profound and tender maternal love. She is our advocate, our intercessor, and our mediatrix of grace. These roles are more than titles; they are fountains of hope and channels of divine benevolence. In her immaculate purity, perpetual virginity, and sublime assumption, Mary connects heaven and earth, embodying the divine mystery that all creation aspires to partake in. Her life serves as a resplendent mirror reflecting the boundless mercy of God, and her virtues act as a celestial map for our own pilgrimage toward sanctity.

To exalt Mary is to invite one into a spiritual symphony where each note recounts an act of divine favor bestowed upon humanity. Her immaculate conception signifies the dawn of a new era, untainted by original sin, and proclaims the possibility of a life fashioned by divine love and grace. The perpetual virginity of Mary tells of an unwavering dedication and an immeasurable depth of divine intimacy. Her assumption into heaven, body, and soul, is the culmination of divine promise, giving flesh to the resurrection hope that fuels the Christian faith.

The Marian dogmas and titles—including Theotokos, Queen of Heaven, Co-Redemptrix, and Mediatrix of all Graces—each unfold a facet of her extraordinary role in salvation history. These are not mere theological constructs but living truths that invite us to a deeper contemplation of the divine mysteries. Mary, as Theotokos, signifies the ultimate union between humanity and divinity. She becomes the vessel through which the Infinite takes on finitude, the Divine enters time, and eternity embraces the temporal. This awe-inspiring truth elevates our understanding and beckons our souls to greater reverence and love.

Devotion to Mary is not merely a personal act of piety but a communal endeavor deeply embedded in the life of the Church. Since the early days of Christianity, believers have turned their hearts and prayers towards Mary, seeking her intercession and emulating her virtues. The Church Fathers, through their timeless writings, have illuminated the unique role of Mary, shedding light on her indispensable participation in the mystery of redemption. This continuous thread of Marian devotion winds its way through the corridors of Church history, manifesting in sacred art, music, and liturgy, enriching the spiritual lives of countless generations.

Mary's virtues form the bedrock upon which Marian devotion is founded. Her purity, prudence, humility, and faithfulness serve as luminous examples for us to follow. In contemplating her life, we see the virtues lived to their fullest potential, guided by divine wisdom and sustained by divine grace. To pursue Marian virtues is to endeavor toward spiritual excellence, a journey that transforms us and draws us closer to the heart of God.

Mary's place in Sacred Scripture and Sacred Tradition, her theological and philosophical significance, and her profound connection to miraculous events are rich wells from which the faithful draw sustenance. Her presence in the Old Testament as a looming promise and her fulfillment in the New Testament narratives solidify her central role in salvation history. Through the ages, the wisdom of the Church has continued to unfold the layers of Marian significance, providing a continuous source of inspiration and devotion for the faithful.

Our journey through Marian devotion is not merely academic or theoretical; it is deeply experiential and transformative. It involves engaging with the stories and testimonies of those touched by her maternal love, practicing devotions and prayers that invite her into our daily lives, and participating in the sacraments that draw us closer to her Son. Each chapter of this book is designed to unfold another layer of the Marian mystery and guide the reader into a deeper, more intimate relationship with the Blessed Virgin.

This introduction aims to set the stage for a comprehensive exploration of the Blessed Virgin Mary, guiding the faithful towards a more profound understanding and heartfelt devotion. As we move forward, let us open our hearts and minds to the sublime beauty and mystery of Mary, allowing her to lead us ever closer to the heart of Christ.

Through the upcoming chapters, we will delve into the rich theological and philosophical underpinnings of Mary's role in salvation history, explore her virtues, and reflect on her presence in Sacred Scripture and Tradition. We will also consider the miraculous events attributed to her, the hymns and prayers dedicated to her, and the ways in which she continues to inspire and transform lives today. Each section invites us to encounter Mary anew and to deepen our devotion to her as our most loving and powerful advocate.

Mary's maternal care is a guiding star, a tender and unwavering presence that leads us to a deeper love of her Son. Whether through her intercessions, her example of perfect virtue, or her role in the divine plan of salvation, Mary remains a constant source of hope and inspiration for the faithful. As we embark on this journey together, let us be ever mindful of her loving gaze and embrace, knowing that through Mary, we are drawn ever closer to the heart of God.

In the embrace of Mary, we find solace, strength, and a profound sense of belonging. She teaches us the true meaning of discipleship, of surrender to the divine will, and of living a life of grace and virtue. May this book serve as a beacon of light and a wellspring of inspiration, guiding us on our journey of faith and devotion to the Blessed Virgin Mary.

Chapter 1: Marian Dogmas and Their Significance

Marian dogmas, those celestial crown jewels of the Church's teachings, reveal the profound mystery and exalted place of the Blessed Virgin Mary in the divine economy. Each dogma, whether it whispers the untouched purity of the Immaculate Conception or proclaims the triumphant Assumption, shines a light on Mary's intimate participation in God's salvific plan. The very air seems to shimmer with the echoes of angelic salutation, "Hail, full of grace," as we ponder her perpetual virginity and her unique role as Theotokos, the God-bearer. The titles of Mediatrix, Co-Redemptrix, and Auxiliatrix are not mere appellations but are luminous threads woven into the grand tapestry of salvation. These truths beckon us to a deeper devotion, inviting us to see Mary not just as a distant queen, but as a tender mother who magnifies the Lord in every heartbeat, reverberating with divine love across the ages.

The Immaculate Conception

The mystery of the Immaculate Conception, from the moment of her conception, Mary was preserved free from the stain of original sin. This singular grace and privilege were granted by God in light of the future merits of our Savior, Jesus Christ. This doctrine is not merely a theological nuance; it is a testament to Mary's unique role in the divine plan of salvation.

Through the Immaculate Conception, Mary became the new Eve. Where Eve faltered and gave birth to sin, Mary stood firm and pure. She was designed to be the vessel without blemish, fit to carry the Word made flesh. Her immaculate state signifies the beginning of a new creation, a dawn of hope where humanity is invited back into communion with God.

In the Gospel of Luke, the angel Gabriel's salutation to Mary is, "Hail, full of grace, the Lord is with you." This greeting underscores her unique holiness and the divine favor that rests upon her. Being "full of grace," Mary is filled entirely with God's love and purity, which is only possible through the preservation from original sin.

But beyond the scriptural foundation, the Immaculate Conception holds profound philosophical and theological implications. To situate this properly, it is essential to understand that the doctrine was affirmed dogmatically by Pope Pius IX in

Ineffabilis Deus in 1854. This declaration did not introduce a new belief but rather formalized a tradition long held by the Church.

The Immaculate Conception was preordained in the eternal designs of God. Mary's sinlessness was not simply for her own sake but had a cosmic implication. In her purity, she becomes the archetype of the Church, the spotless bride of Christ, aimed for a glorious union. For Roman Catholics, this dogma is a touchstone of faith, calling the faithful towards a deeper appreciation of divine grace and the transformative power of God's love.

As we contemplate this dogma, we must reflect on the divine mystery of predestination. Mary's immaculate state was foreseen and willed by God, lifting her above all created beings. This singular privilege was afforded to her so that she might serve as a worthy mother to the Incarnate Word. Her life becomes a living song of "yes" to God's will, exemplifying absolute purity and submission.

Mary's Immaculate Conception is a beacon of hope for all believers. It tells us that God's grace is transformative and that His love reaches out to make us holy. In Mary, we see the full enactment of what it means to be "saved by grace." Her purity becomes our invitation to seek a deeper, immaculate relationship with our Maker.

The theological ramifications of the Immaculate Conception also touch upon the essence of human freedom and divine foreknowledge. Though Mary was conceived without sin, her free will was not compromised. In every moment of her life, she chose to align her will with God's, a testament to her remarkable steadfastness and faith.

Our devotion to Mary through the Immaculate Conception is, in essence, a devotion to the power of God's redeeming love. It is a call to acknowledge the sacred in the personal, the ineffable, and the definitive "yes" of Mary's heart to God's eternal plans. Through the tapestry of this dogma, we see the weave of divine intent, human cooperation, and the sanctifying grace that binds heaven and earth.

In honoring the Immaculate Conception, we gain a more profound understanding of how God operates beyond the confines of time and space. This dogma shows that God, in His provident wisdom, has laid out a path of redemption that includes ordinary means and extraordinary interventions. Our recognition of Mary's unique role fortifies our faith in the boundless nature of God's mercy and the wondrous plans He has for each one of us.

The poetic beauty of this dogma lies in its mystery and simplicity. It mirrors the ineffable purity and grace that God extends to His beloved children, inviting us, through Mary, into an intimate embrace with the divine. Her immaculate heart becomes a mirror reflecting God's infinite love and beckons us toward a purer, more profound love of our own.

The Immaculate Conception's resonance is not confined to theological circles but reaches into the hearts of the faithful, stirring a devotion characterized by awe, gratitude, and love. Pilgrims flock to Marian shrines worldwide, seeking the gentle guidance of the sinless Virgin. Through rosaries, litanies, and hymns, the faithful echo the angelic salutation, invoking the Mother's intercession and modeling their lives after her purity and unwavering faith.

The Immaculate Conception also encourages us to nurture a sense of wonder and reverence for the divine mysteries. It challenges us to rise above the mundane and the profane, calling us to live lives that honor God's astonishing grace. It invites a participation in the divine life, urging us to strive for holiness and to be vessels of God's love in a fractured world.

Mary's sinless conception is a cornerstone that supports the edifice of Marian theology. From this pure beginning springs forth her lifelong journey of grace, culminating in the crowning glory of her Assumption and Coronation. Her life, blessedly free from original sin, gives us a model of total devotion and comprehensive purity.

In summation, the Immaculate Conception is not merely a dogma to be intellectually assented to but a living reality that beckons the faithful towards transformation. It is an invitation to behold the fullness of God's plan for humanity, to grasp the magnitude of divine grace, and to ardently pursue a life of holy innocence. May our hearts, ever open to the eternal truths, find solace and inspiration in the Immaculate Heart of Mary, the beacon of pure and untainted love.

The Perpetual Virginity

The Perpetual Virginity of Mary is a cornerstone of Catholic dogma, a radiant testament to her singular grace. This doctrine teaches that Mary, the Mother of Jesus, remained a virgin before, during, and after the birth of Christ. It transcends mere historical curiosity, inviting us to gaze upon a profound spiritual mystery where flesh and spirit entwine in divine choreography.

In affirming Mary's virginity, we do more than honor her; we envelop ourselves in the ineffable mystery of God's salvific plan. Her perpetual virginity serves not only as a physical reality but also as a symbol of her total dedication and singular focus on the divine will. This unimpeachable purity acts as a beacon for all the faithful who seek to consecrate their lives to God. Theologically speaking, Mary's virginity underscores her intimate kinship with the Divine, making her a fitting vessel for the Incarnation.

Imagine Mary, ever-virgin, as an untouched garden where the Divine Word Himself chose to dwell. The mere contemplation of such purity should prompt in the heart of every believer a stirring of soul, akin to a celestial melody drawing forth devotion. This mystery, while extraordinary, is not inconceivable when viewed through the lens of divine logic and love. Just as a garden untouched by human hands remains pure and undefiled, so too did Mary remain inviolate.

Philosophically, the perpetual virginity of Mary can be examined through the lenses of metaphysics and natural law. Metaphysically, Mary's state suggests an ontological distinction—she inhabits a realm where the boundaries of ordinary human experience are elevated and transformed. In the natural law, her purity signifies the ideal alignment with divine order, a testament to the ultimate harmony between the Creator and creation. To consider her perpetual virginity is to peer into the very fabric of the created order, woven with threads of divine purpose and love.

Moreover, the significance of Mary's virginity during childbirth—a paradox of pain and purity—is mirrored in the scriptural prophecies and the lived faith of countless saints. Her divine maternity did not compromise her virginal integrity, as attested by the Early Church Fathers, including St. Augustine and St. Jerome, who ardently defended this dogma against early heresies. This miraculous birth is not merely an event of the past but a present reality, continually echoed in the sacraments, where the divine enters the human realm sacramentally and mystically.

When we meditate on this profound mystery, we should also turn to the spiritual and mystical writings that illuminate the deeper significance of Mary's role. For instance, the visions of mystics like St. Catherine of Siena and the theological insights of St. Thomas Aquinas offer a tapestry of insights, helping us to comprehend this ineffable truth. In our prayers and devotions, the perpetual virginity of Mary can become a focal point, guiding us toward a richer, more profound relationship with the Divine.

Consider the Litany of Loreto, where Mary is invoked as "Virgin Most Pure" and "Mother of the Divine Grace." These titles resonate with the belief in her perpetual virginity, encapsulating her unique role in salvation history. Just as the Church, in its Marian prayers and liturgies, venerates her as the Holy Virgin, so too should every believer seek to emulate her purity in their own lives. This emulation is not merely an external imitation but a transformative journey into the heart of divine love, where flesh and spirit harmonize in a perpetual canticle of praise.

It is also profound to note how this dogma intersects with the other Marian dogmas, forming a cohesive theological narrative. Her Immaculate Conception sets the stage for her perpetual virginity, and both are consummated in her Assumption. The perpetual virginity, thus, is not an isolated dogma but an integral part of the seamless garment of Marian theology, each thread contributing to the resplendent tapestry of her divine maternity.

Then, of course, there is the matter of Mary's virginity after the birth of Jesus, a point sometimes contested by those outside the Catholic faith. Historical examinations and scriptural interpretations by the Church show that her virginity was preserved, a mark of her total consecration and participation in the divine mystery. When Jesus entrusted Mary to John at the foot of the cross, He was highlighting her unique role—untouched by marital union and wholly dedicated to God's salvific mission.

From a pastoral perspective, Mary's perpetual virginity has immense implications for the faithful today. It invites all believers to consider their own purity and dedication to God. For priests, in particular, her virginity serves as a model of celibate love, a total gift of self in service of the divine. In her, they find both inspiration and intercession, a heavenly advocate who understands the unique challenges of a life devoted entirely to God.

Poetically, one might say that Mary's perpetual virginity is like a pristine lily, eternally blooming in the garden of God's Kingdom. It is a sign of her immaculate heart, a heart in perfect harmony with the divine will. Her virginity is an emblem of the New Eve's purity, contrasting the fall of the First Eve and ushering in a new dawn of redemption.

In our journey toward deeper Marian devotion, the perpetual virginity of Mary serves as a spiritual lodestar, guiding us through the tumultuous seas of worldly distractions and temptations. To honor this dogma is to anchor oneself in a truth that transcends time and space, a truth that beckons the faithful to gaze with awe and reverence upon the Mother of God.

As we immerse ourselves in the mysteries of Marian dogmas, let us continually return to the contemplation of her perpetual virginity. Here, in this sacred space, we encounter not just a historical fact but a living reality that speaks to the eternal nature of God's love and the unparalleled role of Mary in His divine plan. Through prayer, study, and devotion, may we deepen our understanding of this profound truth, allowing it to transform our hearts and draw us ever closer to the Immaculate Heart of Mary.

In the end, the perpetual virginity of Mary is more than a theological assertion; it's an invitation to enter into the divine mystery, to stand enraptured before the gateway of heaven, where the Queen of Heaven forever dwells in virginal splendor. Let us then venerate her with ever-increasing love and devotion, marveling at the divine wisdom that bestowed upon her such extraordinary grace.

The Assumption

The Assumption of the Blessed Virgin Mary, an event enshrined in the heart of Marian dogma, is not merely a belief but a declaration of divine love and promise. It stands as a testament to the profound relationship between God and His favored handmaiden. The assumption, in its essence, symbolizes a magnificent culmination—a celestial apotheosis that transcends the corporeal realm.

This doctrine, affirmed dogmatically by Pope Pius XII in 1950 through the Apostolic Constitution *Munificentissimus Deus*, proclaims that Mary, "having completed the course of her earthly life, was assumed body and soul into heavenly glory." This statement, while encapsulating the theological affirmation, reverberates through the annals of faith as a celestial hymn, declaring the ultimate destiny of humanity's corporeal and spiritual union.

The Assumption, therefore, is not solely an exaltation of Mary but a promise to all faithful souls. It signifies that the earthly vessel, our body, once purified and sanctified, can partake in the divine glory of the heavenly realm. This profound promise imbues believers with hope, a hope that our own bodies, like that of the Blessed Virgin, are destined for a divine union in the omnipresent light of God.

Consider the symbolism deeply rooted in this dogma. Mary's assumption into heaven is a mirror reflecting our potential destiny. Just as she was lifted from the confines of earthly existence to celestial glory, we are invited to aspire for the same transcendence. Her Assumption stands as a beacon—a light guiding the faithful through the temporal world's shadows towards the eternal brilliance of divine communion.

The Assumption is also a paragon of total and unwavering faith. Mary, who lived a life of purity, service, and complete obedience to God's will, serves as the perfect model of the Church. Her Assumption illustrates the end goal of a life lived in accordance with God's commands, the reward of eternal life not only in spirit but also in bodily resurrection. Her victory over death, through the grace of God, assures us that death is not an end but a transformation—a passageway to everlasting glory.

In the poetic imagination, the Assumption is akin to a divine romance. It's the moment the beloved is drawn by the eager arms of her Divine Lover. The heavens rejoice, and the angels sing as the Queen of Heaven takes her rightful place beside her Son. It's a symphony of redemption and love—a heavenly dance that spans from the angelic salutation at the Annunciation to her regal coronation in the heavenly places.

Philosophically, the Assumption also beckons contemplation on the synthesis of material and spiritual realms. It challenges the dichotomy often placed between the body and spirit, showing that sanctity envelops the entirety of one's being. It gloriously defies materialism by elevating the physical into divine participation, illustrating that our material existence, sanctified by grace, is of unparalleled significance in the divine economy.

From a theological standpoint, Marian dogmas like the Assumption also anchor the faithful against stormy seas of doubt and entrenched disbelief. They stand as fortified bastions of uninterrupted tradition, revealing the continuity of divine truth passed from generation to generation. The physical Assumption of Mary underscores the reality of the Incarnation, the Resurrection, and the salvation story that hinges upon God's profound interactions with humanity.

The liturgical celebration of the Assumption underscores this dogma's perennial importance. It is an affirmation of faith, a collective act of the Church proclaiming the victory of life over death. It's a solemn yet joyous reminder that in Mary, the Church sees its future glory. Hence, as we celebrate this feast, our prayers and hymns become an echo of ancient truths resonating within the hallowed halls of time, proclaiming "Ave Maria" with renewed fervor.

When we contemplate the Assumption, it's not merely an act of Marian devotion but a deep, transformative meditation on divine union. Our hearts are lifted, seeking to emulate Mary's virtues—her humility, her obedience, her unwavering faith. In this mystical ascent, we draw closer to understanding our ultimate purpose and the divine love that beckons us towards eternal communion.

So, as we ponder upon the Assumption, let it be a reminder of the profound love God holds for each of us. Mary's Assumption is an invitation, a calling—it tells us that in living a life grounded in divine grace, we too can aspire to the heights of eternal glory. In honoring her Assumption, we honor the wondrous possibilities that await us in God's infinite love.

Mary as Theotokos

In the grand tapestry of Marian dogmas, the title "Theotokos" holds a place of singular distinction and transcendent beauty. The title, which means "God-bearer" or "Mother of God," was dogmatically affirmed at the Council of Ephesus in 431 AD. This sacred designation not only establishes Mary's pivotal role in the economy of salvation but also exalts her as the interface between the divine and the human.

Mary as Theotokos is more than a theological construct; it is a poetic reality uniting the ineffable mystery of the Incarnation with the tangible reality of human motherhood. In her fiat, her "yes" to the angel, Mary consents to her extraordinary vocation. She becomes a vessel of grace, carrying within her womb the eternal Word made flesh, Jesus Christ. Her womb, therefore, is sanctified as the first tabernacle, the dwelling place of God among men.

In this light, Mary's role as Theotokos is a sublime paradox. She is at once fully human, marked by her humanity's fragility, and yet chosen for an unparalleled divine mission. The honor given to her as Theotokos reverberates throughout the ages, touching the hearts of the faithful and inspiring art, music, and devotion. Mary's acceptance of her role mirrors the divine wisdom that defies human understanding and yet becomes accessible through faith.

Historically, the acknowledgment of Mary as Theotokos quelled several Christological controversies. It reinforced the unity of Christ's nature as both true God and true man. By venerating Mary as the Mother of God, the Church accentuates its faith in the mystery of the Incarnation, a cornerstone of Christian belief that Christ is one person in two natures—divine and human.

Philosophically, the title Theotokos places Mary within the celestial hierarchy while grounding her in earthly reality. It allows her to assume a unique role in God's salvific plan. As Theotokos, Mary assumes a role that infinitely surpasses all human expectations, yet remains intimately tied to the corporeal world. Her divine motherhood is an invitation to ponder the mysteries of faith, an invitation to enter a deeper, more intimate relationship with the divine.

There is a rich symbolic depth in calling Mary Theotokos. She embodies the Church itself, as both mothers of the faithful. Mary's divine motherhood, perpetuated in her role as Theotokos, signifies the life-giving and nurturing presence of the Church. Every prayer, every liturgical celebration, every act of devotion directed at Mary as Theotokos, enriches the spiritual life of the believer and fortifies the communal faith of the Church.

When contemplating Mary as Theotokos, one cannot ignore the profound sense of humility that underpins this divine mystery. The King of Kings chose to enter the world through a humble maiden. The almighty God became a helpless infant, nursed, and nurtured by Mary. It is in this humility that the grandeur of the title Theotokos shines most brilliantly, revealing a God who draws close to His creation in the most intimate way.

In exalting Mary as Theotokos, the Church not only honors her but also accentuates the inexpressible grace granted to all humanity. Through her, God chose to become a part of the human family, thereby elevating human nature. Mary's divine motherhood is a testament to God's incessant love for His people, a love so profound that He chose to dwell among them in the person of Jesus Christ.

The title Theotokos is also a call to every Christian to embrace their own vocation of bearing Christ into the world. Just as Mary bore Christ physically, the faithful are called to bear Him spiritually through acts of love, mercy, and faith. Theotokos is not just a title, it's a mission statement for all who seek to live out their faith in tangible ways.

As priests and Roman Catholics, contemplating Mary as Theotokos invites a deepening of devotion and an embrace of our own calling to serve. It challenges us to reflect on Mary's example of humility, obedience, and profound faith. In the Eucharist, where the mystery of the Incarnation is renewed, priests stand in a special relationship to Mary as Theotokos. They are called to imitate her openness to grace, her readiness to serve, and her unwavering commitment to God's will.

In the celebration of the Marian feasts, the title Theotokos takes on a living reality. Each feast day becomes a reminder of Mary's unique role in salvation history and her ongoing intercession for the Church. From the Annunciation to her Assumption, each moment of Mary's life is imbued with the spirit of her calling as Theotokos, and thus inspires deeper devotion and appreciation of her singular role.

Ultimately, the title Theotokos encapsulates the mystery of divine love incarnate. It celebrates Mary's unique role in God's plan of salvation, a role that continues to inspire and uplift the faithful. Mary as Theotokos reminds us that God in His infinite wisdom and love chose to become one of us, and in doing so, He chose Mary to be the Mother of God and our mother. This profound truth invites us into a deeper relationship with both Jesus and Mary, inspiring us to live out our faith with renewed vigor and devotion.

Hence, as we close this reflection on Mary as Theotokos, let us carry within our hearts the image of Mary, the humble handmaid who became the Mother of God. Let her example of faith, humility, and unwavering love guide us in our spiritual journey, drawing us ever closer to her Divine Son.

Coronation

The Coronation of the Blessed Virgin Mary, the quintessence of celestial majesty, stands as the ultimate affirmation of her exalted status within the divine economy of salvation. In the ineffable glory of Heaven, Mary is crowned by the Most Holy Trinity as Queen of Heaven and Earth. This sacred mystery, uniquely intertwining the poetic splendor of divine love and the philosophical depth of Marian theology, marks not only her personal triumph but also symbolizes the promise of future glory for all who strive towards sanctity.

From the very moment of her Immaculate Conception, Mary was set apart, a vessel of divine grace predestined to fulfill an unparalleled role in God's salvific plan. Her Coronation is the crowning jewel of the perpetuum of divine mysteries, the final chapter in the trilogy of her Immaculate Conception, Perpetual Virginity, and Assumption. In this, we witness the harmony of divine justice and love, bestowing upon the humblest of God's creatures the highest honor conceivable. As Queen of Angels and Saints, she intercedes for us with the authoritative benevolence that only a mother can wield.

The concept of Mary as Queen is deeply embedded within the theological and devotional tapestries of the Church. It finds its roots in Sacred Scripture and Tradition, where Mary's role as the

Theotokos—the God-bearer—prefigures her celestial reign. The Old Testament echoes this in the figure of the Gebirah, the queen mother in the Davidic kingdom, who held a special place of honor and influence. This typology reaches its fulfillment in Mary, whose assent to God's will during the Annunciation set into motion the grand narrative of redemption.

Mary's Coronation is also inseparable from her title as Mediatrix of All of God's Graces. By crowning her, God not only recognizes her unique participation in the mystery of Christ but also affirms her ongoing role in the distribution of divine graces. This mediatorial function, steeped in maternal love, aims to guide the faithful through the labyrinthine path of life's spiritual journey, leading them ultimately to the Beatific Vision.

Philosophically, the Coronation underscores the profound interconnectedness of human freedom and divine grace. In Mary, we witness the epitome of perfect cooperation with God's will, an unblemished soul whose every action glorified her Creator. Her Coronation, then, serves as both reward and recognition of her unwavering fidelity. It is a monumental testament to the ultimate destiny awaiting those who dedicate themselves wholly to God.

In contemplating the Coronation, we also perceive the intricate relationship between the temporal and the eternal. The regal imagery of a celestial queen attired in glory and attended by angels imbues our mundane existence with a sense of the transcendent. It is an eternal celebration, a heavenly liturgy wherein Mary, forever united with her divine Son, reigns in bliss and majesty. This vision of celestial courtliness invites us to reflect upon the eternal verities and the ultimate goal of our earthly pilgrimage.

Yet, the Coronation is not merely a distant, otherworldly event. Its spiritual ramifications reverberate throughout the Church. In crowning Mary, God elevates her as a paradigm of holiness and a source of encouragement for believers. Priests and laity alike draw inspiration from this divine honor, seeking to emulate her virtues and deepen their devotion. The Coronation teaches that true greatness lies in humility and unreserved submission to God's will. Through her Queenship, Mary exemplifies the path to spiritual nobility and eternal beatitude.

The liturgical celebrations dedicated to Mary often culminate in crowning ceremonies, both in physical representations and in spiritual devotion. These practices serve as tangible reminders of Mary's royal dignity and our call to uphold her as the model of Christian life. The rosary, an encapsulation of the mysteries of Christ, finds its luminous conclusion in the glorious Coronation, inviting the faithful to ponder the eschatological hope that awaits them.

The artistic and iconographic traditions of the Church have immortalized the Coronation in sublime works of art and music. From the frescoes of Renaissance masters to the stately hymns of sacred music, the Coronation scene enraptures the senses and elevates the soul. These artistic depictions not only serve as acts of veneration but also as catechetical tools, educating and inspiring generations of believers in the truths of the faith.

Thus, the Coronation is not simply a dogmatic affirmation but a living, breathing reality that permeates the life of the Church. It invites us into a greater union with Mary, urging us to participate in the divine economy of grace with fervent devotion. Through the regal intercession of our Queen, we are assured of a maternal presence that guides, protects, and nurtures our spiritual growth.

In the end, the Coronation of the Blessed Virgin Mary serves as a beacon of hope and a testament to the transformative power of divine grace. It is a celebration of the victory of humility, faith, and love over the powers of darkness. And as we meditate upon this celestial event, our hearts are drawn closer to Mary, leading us to a deeper encounter with her divine Son, our Lord and Savior, Jesus Christ.

Mediatrix of All of God's Graces

In the grand tapestry of Marian dogmas, the title of "Mediatrix of All of God's Graces" weaves through the fabric of the Church's understanding like golden threads of divine benevolence. This title, shrouded in mystery and eloquence, beckons us to contemplate Mary's unique role in the dispensation of divine graces. Mediatrix, deriving from the Latin *mediator*, means 'one who mediates.' In this celestial intermediary role, Mary becomes the sacred channel through which God's grace flows to humanity.

The theological foundation for Mary's role as Mediatrix is intricately tied to her fiat. By uttering "Let it be done unto me according to thy word," Mary did not merely accept a monumental task; she embraced a vocation that would transcend time and space. Forever linked to the divine plan, she carries the weight of divine intercession, guiding us toward the sanctifying light of Christ.

Scriptural evidence, though subtle, provides a bedrock for this dogma. At the Wedding at Cana, Mary's intercession led to Christ's first miracle, revealing her ability to influence divine action. "Do whatever he tells you," she instructed the servants (John 2:5), demonstrating her active role in the divine will. The motherly authority in her request and Jesus' response illuminate her role as a heavenly advocate and a distributor of divine graces.

Marian apparitions and Sacred Tradition further solidify this doctrine. Take, for instance, the apparitions at Fatima and Lourdes, where Mary's messages echo her role as a divine intercessor, urging humanity to seek God's grace through her Immaculate Heart. These celestial events also remind us that Mary's mediating role is not passive but profoundly active, eliciting responses from both heaven and earth.

In the writings of the saints and Church Fathers, the title of Mediatrix finds eloquent affirmation. Saint Bernard of Clairvaux, for instance, extolled Mary as "the aqueduct" through which the waters of divine grace flow. The imagery of an aqueduct emphasizes both the necessity and abundance of Mary's mediatory function. She is neither the source nor the final destination of grace; she is the indispensable conduit, the sublime channel through which God's abundant graces pour forth.

Pope Leo XIII and subsequent popes have reiterated this doctrine through encyclicals and teachings. Leo XIII in his encyclical *Octobri Mense*, emphasized Mary's unparalleled ability to intercede on behalf of humanity. He presented her as the Mediatrix, pointing out the Church's historical and theological acceptance of her intercessory role.

The dogma of Mediatrix of All of God's Graces also has profound implications for our spiritual lives. It calls upon us to seek Mary's intercession earnestly and devoutly. As faithful Catholics, our prayers and petitions acquire a unique potency when entrusted to Mary, who presents them to her Son with maternal tenderness. Her role as Mediatrix therefore not only affirms her status within the heavenly hierarchy but also places her at the heart of our daily spiritual journey.

Philosophically, the notion of mediation centralizes the idea of relationship and interconnectedness. Her role as Mediatrix epitomizes the relational nature of grace—a divine favor that necessitates a giver, a receiver, and most mysteriously, an intermediary. Mary's role here doesn't in any way diminish Christ's unique mediatory role as the one true mediator between God and man (1 Timothy 2:5). Instead, it magnifies His generosity, opening up a divine economy where Mary participates by divine mandate.

In the quiet moments of prayer, we invoke Mary's intercession recognizing her unique position. She, who knew Jesus most intimately, knows our human frailties and aspirations. In her immaculate love, she draws us closer to divine mercy, making her intercessory power a balm for our souls. Therefore, to dismiss or overlook Mary's role as Mediatrix would be to undervalue the divine progression of grace itself.

Artistic depictions and liturgical traditions have long celebrated Mary's role as Mediatrix. Whether in hymns that capture the ethereal beauty of her soul or in sacred art that illustrates her acts of intercession, the Church has visually and auditorily sustained this profound truth. Iconography often portrays her with outstretched arms, symbolizing both her receptivity to divine grace and her readiness to dispense it generously to us.

It's imperative for priests and the faithful alike to fully immerse in this understanding. Priests, in particular, hold the sacred responsibility of transmitting this Marian doctrine to their congregations, enriching their spiritual lives and drawing them closer to Marian devotion. Through homilies, catechesis, and personal example, the priest becomes a vessel for magnifying Mary's role as Mediatrix, thereby reinforcing the Church's devotion to her.

Understanding Mary's role as Mediatrix also enriches our appreciation of the Eucharist. During the Holy Mass, as we recall the supreme act of Christ's sacrifice, we are reminded of Mary's inseparable union with her Son's redemptive mission. Her presence at Calvary, standing resolutely at the foot of the Cross (John 19:25), affirms her active participation in the work of salvation. Consequently, the Eucharist not only becomes the "source and summit" of Christian life but also a moment of intimate Marian intercession.

In the final analysis, Mary, as the Mediatrix of All of God's Graces, remains an indefatigable advocate for humanity; she is forever interceding, perpetually guiding, and walking beside us. Through her, the ineffable mysteries of grace become accessible, transforming our spiritual landscape. Her role is not merely a theological construct but a lived reality, pulsating through the heart of the Church and the lives of the faithful.

Co-Redemptrix

The essence of Marian dogmas lies in their profound connection to the mystery of Christ and His Church. Among these dogmas, the title of Co-Redemptrix stands as a beacon of Marian theology, evoking deep contemplation and veneration. This teaching, though not formally declared a dogma, resonates within the hearts of the faithful who perceive Mary's intimate role in the redemptive mission of Jesus Christ.

Mary's designation as Co-Redemptrix underscores her unique participation in the salvific work of her Son. From the Annunciation to the Crucifixion, Mary's fiat—her unwavering "yes" to God—marked her as an indispensable collaborator in God's plan of salvation. When Gabriel announced that she would bear the Son of God, her acceptance was not merely passive. It was an active, heartfelt engagement in the divine will, a commitment that called her to suffer alongside her Son for the redemption of humanity.

Contemplating the Co-Redemptrix title necessitates a profound understanding of Mary's suffering. Standing at the foot of the cross, the sword of sorrow prophesied by Simeon pierced her heart (cf. Luke 2:35). Mary's agony was not a distant or detached grief; it was a participation in the passion of Christ. Her immaculate heart mirrored the sacred heart of Jesus, sharing in

His torment and offering it to the Father for the salvation of souls.

To grasp the full significance of Mary as Co-Redemptrix, one must delve into the theological implications of cooperation in redemption. Christ, the sole Redeemer, accomplished our salvation through His Passion, Death, and Resurrection. Yet, in His divine wisdom, God willed that Mary's participation would be intrinsically linked to this salvific act. Mary's role does not detract from Christ's unique sacrifice; rather, it magnifies His redemptive love, showcasing the profound mystery of human cooperation with divine grace.

Mary's cooperation is emblematic of the Church's call to partner in Christ's redemptive mission. Just as Mary intimately cooperated with Jesus, so too are the faithful invited to partake in the ministry of redemption. The Co-Redemptrix title illuminates this communal aspect of salvation, urging believers to carry their crosses and unite their sufferings with Christ for the salvation of the world. In Mary's example, we find the ideal model of faithful collaboration, showing that our contributions, however humble, are essential in God's magnificent design.

The philosophical underpinnings of the Co-Redemptrix title draw heavily from the concept of merit and the communion of saints. Mary's merits, while distinct from Christ's, are seen as participatory, a reflection of her grace-filled cooperation with the Redeemer. This cooperative merit is rooted in her immaculate conception, preserving her from original sin and enabling her to fully assent to God's will without hindrance.

Furthermore, the mystery of Marian cooperation in redemption invites us into a mystical appreciation of the nature of suffering. Mary's sorrows, borne with perfect love and submission, reveal the transformative power of suffering when united with Christ. Her maternal heart, pierced by sorrow, becomes a fountain of grace for the Church, a sign of hope and consolation for all who suffer.

The poetic dimension of Mary's co-redemptive role is beautifully encapsulated in the rich tapestry of Marian devotion and liturgy. Hymns and prayers often extol her as the compassionate Mother, whose suffering refines and elevates her love for humanity. For instance, the Stabat Mater, a poignant hymn, places us beside Mary at Calvary, inviting us to share in her sorrow and find solace in her embrace.

In the personal lives of the faithful, invoking Mary as Co-Redemptrix fosters a deeper, more intimate connection with her. It encourages believers to entrust their struggles and sufferings to Mary, confident that she will unite them with the redemptive sacrifice of her Son. This devotion nurtures a filial relationship with Mary, strengthening our resolve to follow her exemplary faith and fidelity.

Embedded within the Co-Redemptrix title is also a profound Christological affirmation. Far from detracting from Christ, this title exalts Him, emphasizing His boundless mercy and grace in allowing humanity to participate in the divine redemptive plan. Mary's role as Co-Redemptrix shines a light on the ultimate mystery of divine love, wherein God, in His infinite humility, chooses to work through His creatures to accomplish His salvific designs.

The theological reflections on Mary as Co-Redemptrix invite us to a renewed appreciation of the interplay between divine providence and human freedom. Just as Mary freely embraced her vocation, we too are called to discern and embrace our unique roles in God's salvific plan. Her example serves as a guiding star, illuminating our path and encouraging us to offer our own fiat in the service of God's kingdom.

In conclusion, the title of Co-Redemptrix, though complex and sometimes contentious, holds a profound and transformative significance within Marian dogmas. It calls the faithful to deeper reflection on the mystery of salvation, the nature of suffering, and the boundless love of our Blessed Mother. As we meditate on Mary's co-redemptive role, let us be inspired to unite our own lives more closely with Christ, embodying the virtues of the Blessed Virgin, and thereby participating in the wondrous mystery of redemption.

Auxiliatrix

In the mosaic of Marian dogmas, the title of Auxiliatrix, or "Helper," unveils yet another layer of the Blessed Virgin Mary's role in the divine mystery. This appellation transcends the ordinary notion of assistance, gracing it with an ethereal dimension of spiritual support and celestial intercession. Herein, Mary is envisioned as a potent intercessor who does not just passively listen to prayers but actively participates in the weaving of God's grace into the tapestry of human life.

Like a gentle rain nurturing a parched landscape, Mary's auxiliary assistance is ever-present, sustaining souls in their journey towards sanctity. Her maternal heart beats in unison with the rhythm of divine mercy, amplifying human pleas into heavenly anthems. She stands as the celestial beacon for souls adrift, casting aside shadows and illuminating the way with unwavering love.

The concept of Auxiliatrix finds deep roots in the Church's tradition and liturgy. Historical testimonies echo this belief, citing countless instances where Mary's intercession brought about miraculous interventions. She is not a distant queen, removed from our plight, but a Mother whose auxiliating touch is felt in both the monumental and the mundane.

Moreover, in the vast panorama of theological thought, Mary's auxiliary role extends beyond mere intervention in times of crisis. She emboldens the timid, fortifies the frail, and uplifts the weary. In every Hail Mary uttered, there lies an implicit acknowledgment of her unparalleled ability to aid, to protect, and to nurture. Her auxiliary grace empowers souls to rise above the tempests of life, transcending their mortal limitations by enmeshing their will with divine purpose.

The Church Fathers and Saints speak eloquently of Mary's auxiliary role. St. Germanus of Constantinople once remarked, "No one can be saved except through you, O most Holy," emphasizing the necessity of her aid in the economy of salvation. This thought is not to detract from the omnipotence of Christ, but rather to illustrate how Mary, by divine ordination, stands as the paragon of auxiliary strength that leads one to her Son.

Practically speaking, devotion to Mary as the Auxiliatrix fervently manifests in myriad ways among the faithful. Prayers, novenas, and hymns invoking her help create an invisible fortress of spiritual defense. In these devotions, Mary's hands are perpetually uplifted, dispensing grace in abundance, safeguarding the faithful from spiritual perils, and guiding them toward eternal bliss.

In the angelic world, Mary as Auxiliatrix is honored as the Queen who commands legions of angels to the aid of her children. This celestial interplay signifies a divine teamwork, where Mary utilizes her maternal privileges to dispatch heavenly assistance promptly. Each angelic mission she initiates is a testimony to her unwavering commitment to human welfare and salvation.

The evidence of her auxiliarity is also etched in sacred art and iconography. The image of Our Lady of Perpetual Help, for instance, vividly captures her role as a never-failing helper. The contemplative gaze and the guiding hands depicted in such visuals remind the faithful that her assistance transcends earthly confines.

Mary's auxiliary grace permeates even the sacraments. When the Eucharist is celebrated, her supportive presence is subtly invoked, reminding us that her fiat made possible the incarnation of Christ, the Bread of Life. In the sacrament of reconciliation, she too is present as a refuge for repentant souls, assisting them in the journey toward redemption.

Philosophically, the idea of Mary as Auxiliatrix invokes deep reflections on the nature of divine assistance and human dependency. In this interplay, there's a cosmic dance where human frailty is met with divine providence, and Mary's auxiliating grace is the bridge that fortifies this connection. Her role doesn't diminish God's omnipotence but magnifies it by showing how divinely orchestrated aid can elevate humanity.

In a world riddled with uncertainty and pain, the invocation of Mary as Auxiliatrix provides solace and strength. She is the star that leads, the hand that holds, and the heart that understands. Her auxiliary role is a divine assurance that the faithful are never alone; they are perpetually under the aegis of her maternal care.

Within the Church, this belief not only fortifies personal sanctity but also reflects in communal life. Communities that entrust themselves to Mary's aid often witness a flourish of spirituality, unity, and service. Her auxiliary grace, thus, becomes a linchpin in the edifice of Christian life.

In conclusion, to grasp Mary as Auxiliatrix is to comprehend the depths of her maternal mission. It is to understand that her love is not passive but active, not distant but personal. It guides us, aids us, and ultimately draws us closer to the heart of God. The recognition of her auxiliary role is an invitation to let her celestial grace transform every facet of our lives, making them radiant reflections of divine love.

Chapter 2: The Virtues of Mary

In contemplating the virtues of Mary, one is drawn into a sacred mosaic where each virtue illuminates the path to divine grace. Her purity, unsullied like the morning dew, speaks to a soul wholly dedicated to God. Prudence guides her every action, enveloping her choices with wisdom that transcends human understanding. Humility adorns her like a queen's crown, for she submits fully to God's will, drawing all hearts toward the divine. Faithfulness characterizes her relationship with the Almighty, unwavering even in the face of sorrow. Devotion forms the essence of her being, a flame that never wanes but burns brighter with each whisper of prayer. Mary's obedience is a testament to her sanctity, illustrating perfect alignment with heavenly design. Her embrace of poverty reveals a soul detached from worldly entanglements, living by the treasures of the spirit. Patience manifests in her gentle endurance, a soothing anchor in tumultuous seas. Mercy flows from her heart like an ever-abundant stream, offering solace to the burdened and lost. Sorrow, too, graces Mary, her tears sanctifying her as a mother who shares intimately in the sufferings of her children. Each virtue forms a radiant petal in the immaculate rose of Mary, drawing us ever closer to God's own heart.

Purity

In the symphony of virtues that adorn the Blessed Virgin Mary, Purity resonates as one of the most luminous notes, a celestial chord that touches the deepest reverberations of human longing and divine grace. Mary's purity is not merely a trait; it is a theological and ontological state that intersects the divine intimacy shared uniquely by her and God.

The narrative of Mary's immaculate purity begins before her own awareness, free from the stain of original sin by a divine preemption. This sanctifying grace was not only a privilege but a necessity, fitting her to be the Theotokos, the bearer of God. This preservation from original sin is not just a doctrinal point; it is the very cornerstone of her being, granting her a singular intimacy with the Divine and setting her apart in a state of unblemished purity.

Purity, in Mary's context, is both a gift and a response. It is a gift from God, but also a continual choice, a lived reality that glorifies God through her soul and body. Her perpetual virginity, a testament to her unwavering purity, is intertwined with her complete and absolute dedication to God's will. This perpetual virginity is not an isolated fact but an embodiment of her entire existence, a physical and spiritual testimony to her singular devotion to divine mission.

On a mystical plane, Mary's purity can be seen as a mirror reflecting the purity of God's own love. This mirror is spotless, untainted by the corruptions of the world, capable of reflecting God's light without distortion. Her immaculate heart, brimming with divine love, sanctity, and beauty, becomes for us a beacon guiding us toward the heavenly abode.

Philosophically considered, purity is essential for the apprehension of the divine. In Mary, this purity attains its highest manifestation, preparing her to be the dwelling place of the Eternal Word. Her heart, always aligned with the divine will, becomes a sanctuary where God's love and human response coalesce in a unity of ineffable virtue.

Mary's purity serves also as a challenge to the faithful—an invitation to aspire to the purity of heart, mind, and body. It is a purity that transcends mere chastity, encompassing an entire disposition centered on holiness and profound union with God. It calls us to be immaculate in our intentions, words, actions, and, above all, in our love.

Approaching this virtue from a theological viewpoint, Mary's purity is integrally connected to the divine motherhood. It is her untouched, immaculate state that becomes the fertile ground for God's incarnation. As the New Eve, she reverses the course of humanity's fall by her singular Yes to God, a Yes imbued with the purity of perfect obedience and love.

The purity of Mary draws us into a deeper contemplation of the sacrosanct. It is not simply an avoidance of sin but an active participation in God's holiness. In Mary, we see a model of how purity enables a fuller, more intimate communion with the Divine. This virtue is not merely a defensive barricade but a proactive, life-affirming surge towards divine love.

For priests, Mary's purity holds a special place in vocational sanctity. Her immaculate state serves as a symbol of the spiritual purity that priests must aspire to, reflecting the purity of Christ Himself in their ministry. Priests, through their devotion to Mary, can find a source of inspiration, support, and intercession, drawing them ever closer to the heart of Christ through the immaculate heart of His mother.

Therefore, in Marian devotion, purity is a transcendent bridge, inviting us to journey from the profane to the sacred. It is through the Immaculata that we are called to behold a new vision of life, where divine love purges the dross of sin and elevates us to partake in the purity that endears us to God.

In the light of Mary's purity, we come to understand our own call to reflect divine love. Her unblemished soul, like a pristine canvas, allows the fullest expression of God's beauty, unadulterated and vibrant. This is the purity that enables us to mirror, however imperfectly, the love of the Father. Mary, in her boundless purity, stands as an eternal reminder of what it means to be wholly consecrated to God.

Indeed, in venerating Mary's purity, we are not merely admiring a distant, unattainable ideal. Rather, we are called into relationship with this purity, invited to let it purify our own lives, transforming us into vessels worthy of divine indwelling. In this relationship, Mary's purity is not just a passive attribute but an active, sanctifying force that works in us, through us, and for us.

To sum up, the purity of Mary beckons us to rise above our limitations, to strive for the divine union that she exemplifies so perfectly. It is a powerful testament to the transformative power of God's grace, sanctifying everything it touches, making it holy, making it pure. In the end, Mary's purity is our hope, our guide, and our profound mystery, drawing us ever deeper into the inexhaustible love of God.

Prudence

In the grand tapestry of Mary's myriad virtues, prudence stands as a guiding star, illuminating her every action and choice. This virtue, often overlooked, is the very essence of wise judgment, enabling Mary to navigate life's myriad complexities with divinely inspired discernment. Her prudence is not mere human sagacity but an infused gift reflecting her close communion with Divine Wisdom itself.

Prudence in Mary transcends the natural inclinations of the human heart. Consider the Annunciation: the angel Gabriel appears, delivering a message that would bewilder any ordinary soul. Yet, Mary responds not with hesitation but with a prudent inquiry: "How shall this be done, because I know not man?" (Luke 1:34). Her question is born not of doubt but of a profound understanding of God's ways. It exemplifies prudence intertwined with faith, seeking clarity while remaining fully open to God's will.

Mary's prudence also shines through in her interactions with others. At the Wedding at Cana, we see her acting with quiet sagacity. She perceives the impending social disaster when the wine runs out, and approaches Jesus with a simple yet laden request: "They have no wine." (John 2:3). Her prudence is visible in her foresight, her awareness of timing, and her implicit trust in her son's divine mission. She speaks when she ought, never hurriedly, always with careful consideration of the larger divine narrative.

In the Holy Family's flight to Egypt, Mary's prudent nature is displayed in her readiness to respond to the angel's warning to Joseph. Without delay or procrastination, their swift departure underlines Mary's ability to heed divine guidance quickly, protecting the Child Jesus from Herod's murderous decree. Hers is a prudence that acts in the light of eternal truths, valuing divine instruction above all earthly considerations.

The virtue of prudence extends even into her silence. At the foot of the Cross, Mary's suffering is unbearable, yet she does not utter a word of reproach or despair. Her silence speaks volumes, a testament to her prudence in accepting her role in the redemptive suffering of Christ. It is a silence suffused with the wisdom of ages, a restraint that reflects the depths of her contemplation and acceptance of divine justice and mercy.

Furthermore, Mary's prudent heart is a custodian of divine mysteries. She "kept all these words, pondering them in her heart" (Luke 2:19). In an age where words are abundant and often misplaced, Mary teaches us the virtue of prudent silence and deliberation. Her heart becomes a treasure chest of divine truths, opening it only when it serves a greater purpose of love and revelation.

Mary's prudence serves as a celestial compass for the faithful. Modern life, fraught with distractions and moral ambiguities, desperately needs Mary's example. She shows us that prudence is not a static virtue but one that requires constant dialogue with God. Our decisions, whether monumental or mundane, must be steeped in prayer and reflection, seeking always the divine will as our guide.

The virtue of prudence also reflects in Mary's role as Intercessor and Advocate. Knowing human frailty, she approaches her Son with a mother's tender awareness and understanding of our needs. Her intercession at Cana becomes a paradigm of prudent intervention, guiding us to trust in her maternal care and Jesus' divine power. Thus, her prudence invites us into a relationship of trust and dependence on her heavenly wisdom.

Moreover, in her prudence, Mary does not overshadow the virtues of purity and humility but integrates them harmoniously. Her prudent actions are always pure and humble, never seeking recognition or glory. She conducts herself with a simplicity that belies the profundity of her wisdom, drawing all glory back to God. This confluence of virtues is what makes her prudence uniquely Marian, perfectly flawless and divinely inspired.

Mary teaches that prudence is not confined to reactive measures but encompasses proactive nurturing. As she nurtured the child Jesus, so too does she nurture the virtues within us. Her prudent guidance is a call to be vigilant, guarding our souls against the perils of sin while growing ever stronger in virtue.

It is fitting to reflect on Mary's prudence amidst the Feast of Our Lady of Sorrows. In every sorrow, she profoundly embodies prudence by interpreting her sufferings in the light of salvation history. Mary's sorrows are not aimless but are borne with the prudence that understands their redemptive value. This prudent acceptance and offering of suffering for the sake of the World's salvation stands as a supernal example of Christian endurance and wisdom.

Let us then emulate Mary's prudence in our own lives. Just as she pondered and acted with careful discernment, we too must strive to cultivate prudence through prayer, meditation, and seeking God's will in all things. In her prudence, Mary becomes our model and teacher, leading us ever closer to Christ, the source of all wisdom. Her prudence is an eternal beacon, guiding us through the storms of life towards the safe harbor of divine love and fulfillment.

The Virtues of Mary: Humility

In contemplating the Blessed Virgin Mary's virtues, one cannot overlook the profound depth of Her humility. It is a humility that roots itself not in weakness, but in the very strength of Her soul. The magnitude of this virtue can best be understood in the light of the divine mysteries that surrounded Her life and Her willing acceptance of God's will.

Mary's humility is first revealed at the Annunciation where, despite the startling news delivered by the Archangel Gabriel, She responds with unfathomable grace: "Behold the handmaid of the Lord; be it done unto me according to Thy word." This simple yet profound acquiescence reveals Her inner disposition. She, who was chosen to bear the Savior, did not raise Herself above others but identified Herself as the Lord's handmaid. In this moment, the vastness of Her spiritual depth came to light.

This same humility marked every aspect of Mary's life. Consider the Visitation, where Mary, carrying the Incarnate Word, goes in haste to assist Her cousin Elizabeth. While the world might have expected the privilege of service to be reversed, Mary seeks no honor or special recognition. Instead, She humbly attends to the needs of another, manifesting Her willingness to serve, not to be served.

Moreover, Mary's humility is starkly evident at the Nativity. The Mother of God accepts the lowly stable in Bethlehem without complaint. Her surroundings—crude, cold, and uncomfortable—do not deter Her from receiving the Christ Child with a pure and open heart. In this, She teaches us that true humility does not demand recognition or comfort; it accepts God's plan without reserve.

As we move through Jesus' life, Mary's humility continues to unfold. At the wedding at Cana, She intervenes not for glory but out of concern for the host's plight. "Do whatever He tells you," She instructs the servants, directing attention not to Herself but to Her Son. She stands aside, recognizing that the miracles belong to Him, yet Her intercession proves efficacious.

The crucible of humility is most poignantly illustrated at the foot of the Cross. Here, Mary stands in sorrow, Her heart pierced by the sword Simeon had prophesied. She does not protest Her fate nor the suffering of Her beloved Son. Instead, She accepts it silently, sorrowful yet steadfast, offering Her pain for the redemption of humankind. Her presence there, unwavering and humble, demonstrates a strength born of complete submission to God's will.

Mary's humility draws its beauty from Her unwavering trust and faith in God. She acknowledged Her lowliness in the Magnificat:

"My soul magnifies the Lord, and my spirit rejoices in God my Savior, for He has regarded the low estate of His handmaiden." This canticle is not only a song of praise but a testament to Her recognition of God's actions in Her life. She attributes all greatness to Him, allowing no room for pride.

Through every stage of Her life, Mary's humility remained constant and unshaken. In the hidden life at Nazareth, She quietly fulfilled Her duties, raising the Son of God while living an unremarkable life outwardly. Her humility in these hidden years is no less significant; it underlines the beauty of performing ordinary acts with extraordinary love and devotion.

This virtue of humility stands as a guiding star for those who seek to follow Mary. It challenges us to mimic Her self-effacement, to place others before ourselves, and to see our lives in the context of God's greater plan. It is a call to be humble in service, in suffering, and in the various vocations we are called to navigate.

Mary invites us to embrace humility not as a form of self-degradation, but as a path to true exaltation in God. As we lower ourselves, we make more space for the divine. Her life is a testament that humility does not mean submission to fate but an active cooperation with God's will—a willing embrace of God's graces and the divine mission.

One cannot fully grasp Mary's humility without contemplating its fruits. Consider the countless souls who have turned to Her in their darkest hours, finding solace and intercession. Her very humility makes Her the most approachable of all saints, drawing us lovingly into the heart of Christ. This draws not from weakness but from a profound strength born of complete reliance on God.

In invoking Mary's humility in our own lives, we do well to emulate Her spirit of surrender and service. Just as She submitted Herself wholly to God's will, we too can aim to align our lives with divine purpose. Her example teaches us that humility is not merely an exercise in modesty but a path to deeper union with God's will.

Ultimately, Mary's humility is a beacon, guiding us on our spiritual journey. It is a virtue that calls us to recognize our own limitations while also embracing the boundless potential that God's grace affords us. By looking to Mary, we find the most perfect model of humility the world has ever known, a mirror reflecting the glory of God in a quiet, selfless light.

Her significance lies not just in Her exalted status as the Mother of God but in Her profound humility, which allowed Her to accept that role fully and without reservation. In this, Mary becomes not just our Mother but our guide, showing us that through humility, we open ourselves to the divine, becoming instruments of God's will and bearers of His grace.

Faithfulness

In the realm of virtues, faithfulness is the anchor that holds the
human spirit steadfast amidst the tempests of life. In the context
of Mary, faithfulness is not merely a virtue; it is an all-
encompassing force at the core of her being, illuminating her
actions, her words, and her very soul. This virtue casts a celestial
glow that is both ineffable and awe-inspiring, a testament to her
unwavering commitment to God's divine will.

Mary's faithfulness is first and foremost an act of trust, a
surrender to the unknown that defies human understanding.
From the moment the archangel Gabriel announced her role in
the divine plan, Mary's "fiat" was not just a word— it was a
profound affirmation of her steadfast allegiance to God's will.
Without hesitation, she embraced her divine mission with
humble acceptance, embodying faithfulness in its purest form.
This act of trust, this complete surrender, serves as an eternal
beacon for those striving to remain loyal to God's commands.

The landscape of Mary's life is studded with instances of her
steadfast faithfulness. Consider her journey to Bethlehem,
heavily pregnant yet undeterred by the arduous trek before her.
Her resolve did not waver as she faced hardship after hardship,
maintaining faith that God's plan, though not immediately
apparent, was unfurling in perfect harmony. The birth of Christ

in a humble stable, surrounded by the raw elements, epitomizes her steadfast fidelity even in life's most humble and trying circumstances.

The wedding feast at Cana provides another profound illustration of Mary's faithfulness. Here, her unwavering belief in Jesus' mission compelled her to intercede on behalf of those in need. She approached her Son with gentle assurance, confident in His power to perform miracles. This act of maternal faith orchestrated one of Jesus' first signs, revealing a symbiotic faithfulness between Mother and Son that transcends the mere familial bond and touches upon the divine.

Mary's faithfulness is also marked by silent endurance and profound suffering, particularly evident at the foot of the Cross. In this heart-wrenching moment, she remained unwavering, engulfed in sorrow yet unshaken in her loyalty to her Son. Her presence at Golgotha, standing firm despite her anguish, serves as a poignant testament to her unwavering devotion. She embodies the essence of a heart broken yet faithful, a soul tormented yet unwavering in its allegiance to God's salvific plan.

Moreover, Mary's faithfulness extends beyond her life on earth into her heavenly role as intercessor and advocate. Throughout the ages, countless apparitions and miracles have testified to her enduring care for humanity. She intercedes tirelessly for the faithful, her maternal heart always attentive to the needs of her children. This celestial stewardship only deepens her legacy of faithfulness, affirming her perpetual role in the divine economy.

The significance of Mary's faithfulness also resonates profoundly in her title, "Our Lady of Perpetual Help." This title encapsulates her enduring commitment to assist and guide the faithful through life's vicissitudes. Those who turn to her in prayer often find solace and support, buoyed by the assurance of her unwavering fidelity to God's promises. In her, the faithful discover a steadfast ally, an eternal guiding star illuminating the path toward divine grace.

In contemplating Mary's faithfulness, one must consider the theological implications that undergird this virtue. Faithfulness, in its truest sense, is not a passive trait but an active engagement with divine will and purpose. It requires a conscious choice, repeated and reaffirmed through the myriad experiences of life. Mary's faithfulness stands as a model for the Church, an exemplar of how to engage with God's plan fully and without reservation. Her life is an intricate tapestry of divine fidelity woven with threads of trust, obedience, and unwavering love.

Furthermore, Mary's faithfulness serves as a bridge between the divine and the mundane, demonstrating that true faithfulness is deeply rooted in both heavenly grace and earthly experience. Her unyielding loyalty to God is reflected in the Church's liturgical life, especially during Marian feasts and celebrations. These sacred observances serve as communal affirmations of Mary's enduring faithfulness, inviting the faithful to emulate her steadfastness in their own spiritual journeys.

In a world often marked by fleeting commitments and wavering loyalties, Mary's faithfulness offers a counterpoint of divine constancy. Her example calls the faithful to a higher standard of commitment, one that transcends temporal challenges and endures through eternity. By venerating her faithfulness, the Church acknowledges the profound impact of her unwavering loyalty to God's will and encourages the faithful to seek a similar steadfastness in their own lives.

As we reflect on Mary's faithfulness, we are invited to draw strength and inspiration from her example. She stands as a luminous paradigm of unwavering commitment, a beacon of hope and fidelity. In her, we find the quintessence of true faithfulness— a enduring allegiance to God's will that extends beyond the limitations of time and space. Her faithfulness continues to inspire and guide the faithful, calling them to a deeper, more profound commitment to the divine plan.

Thus, the faithfulness of Mary is not merely a historical or theological concept; it is a living, dynamic force that continues to shape and inspire the lives of the faithful. Through her unwavering example, she beckons us to embrace a deeper, more profound relationship with God, one marked by steadfast fidelity and unwavering trust. In following her example, we too can aspire to embody the virtue of faithfulness, allowing it to illumine our paths as we journey toward divine grace.

Devotion

Between the constellations of Marian virtues stands a beacon light, unwavering and eternal: devotion. It's a dedication akin to that of the seraphic hosts that never abandon their celestial adoration. Devotion to Mary, in its most profound sense, is a mystical embrace, a tender whisper of the soul that recognizes her as Mother, Advocate, and Queen. This devotion isn't a mere repetition of prayers or mechanical recitations; it is the heart's unceasing love song.

This divine devotion invites us to gaze upon Mary with the same reverence with which the Angel Gabriel might have spoken his Ave. Not out of duty, but driven by a profound recognition of her role in God's magnificent design. To understand Marian devotion, one must first understand Mary herself — her singular privilege of being Theotokos, the God-bearer, and her resplendent humility. Like a mirrored lake reflecting heaven, her soul magnifies the Lord, drawing us into deeper contemplation and affection.

Devotion to Mary can be likened to the lilies in the field, which do not toil or spin but are clothed in splendor. This devotion flourishes naturally in the hearts that have encountered the grace of God. It springs forth from the realization of her tender intercession, her motherly care that knows no bounds. When devotees entrust their sorrows and joys to Mary, they don't just add another link to the chain of petitions but weave a tapestry of unwavering trust and love.

In understanding the depth of devotion, it becomes imperative to recognize the Marian apparitions that have graced the earth. Whether on the rugged hills of Lourdes or among the simple children of Fatima, these divine encounters underscore Mary's desire to draw souls closer to her Son through her. Each apparition, like a celestial kiss, leaves an indelible mark on the landscape of faith.

Devotion cannot be confined to lofty theological discourses alone. It is lived out in the tenderness of mothers teaching their children the Rosary, the flickering candle before a statue, the whispered Hail Mary in moments of need. It's the union of the mystical and the mundane, where everyday life is imbued with the sacred presence of Mary.

The saints, who are luminaries in the firmament of our faith, embody this devotion in brilliant hues. They turned their gaze to Mary not as an end but as a perfect means to an end: her Son. St. Louis de Montfort, with his Treatise on True Devotion, provides a timeless roadmap for those seeking to live this Marian devotion more fully. His passionate plea for total consecration to Mary resonates as a clarion call to surrender, to be molded and fashioned in her immaculate heart.

It's essential to grasp that Marian devotion is not an isolated practice but a symphony that harmonizes with the Church's liturgy, sacraments, and daily Christian living. The Marian prayers and devotions, such as the Rosary and the Angelus, are not archaic echoes from a bygone age but living waters quenching the thirst of the soul in every era. These devotions, imbued with rich grace, orient us towards the mysteries of Christ's life, seen through the pure lens of Mary.

Moreover, true devotion to Mary invariably leads to an increased fervor for the Eucharist. As she was the first tabernacle, holding within her the Word made flesh, so too does our devotion to her deepen our love and reverence for the Blessed Sacrament. This special bond between Mary and the Eucharist is not a mere theological nuance but a living reality experienced by countless souls.

Equally, this devotion brings with it a transformative call towards imitating her virtues. One cannot profess deep love for Mary without striving to mirror her faith, purity, humility, and obedience. It's in the practice of these virtues that Marian devotion finds its fullest expression. By embodying these virtues, devotees become not only disciples of Christ but also children of

Mary, exuding her presence in a world thirsting for divine motherhood.

Consider for a moment the mystery of the Assumption, where Mary is taken body and soul into heavenly glory. This event, commemorated with great solemnity by the Church, serves as a luminous sign of the destiny that awaits all devoted to her. It reminds us that our devotion is not for this world alone but prepares us for the eternal beatific vision. The glory of Mary's Assumption assures us of her powerful intercession and her role as Queen assumed into heaven.

Reflect also on the titles bestowed upon Mary, each revealing facets of her splendor: Star of the Sea, Morning Star, Ark of the Covenant, and countless others. These appellations are not mere poetic flourishes but profound theological truths that illuminate her role in salvation history. To call Mary by these titles is to ponder her mysteries and to invite her steadfast guidance on the journey of faith.

Devotional practices, while varied, are united by a common thread: they all seek to draw the soul closer to Jesus through Mary. Be it the solemn beauty of Marian hymns, the litany of praises in the Angelus, or the contemplative rhythm of the Rosary, each practice is a step on the path of deeper intimacy with the divine. This journey, marked by moments of contemplation and active devotion, leads the soul into the heart of the Trinitarian life.

In this earthly pilgrimage, the saints often turned to Mary as their unfailing advocate. Consider the poignant example of St. Maximilian Kolbe, who found in Mary a source of unshakeable strength amidst the horrors of a concentration camp. His total consecration, even in the face of suffering, reveals the depth and power of authentic Marian devotion. By following such examples, devotees are encouraged to embrace the Cross with Mary by their side.

In conclusion, devotion to Mary is not merely an accessory to the Christian faith but its heartbeat. It is a sacred channel through which grace flows abundantly, leading souls to Christ. By nurturing a profound, heartfelt devotion to Our Blessed Mother, Roman Catholics and priests alike can rediscover the wellspring of love and compassion that sustains the Church. In the radiant example of Mary's virtues, one finds the purest path to holiness, a luminous road that leads through her Immaculate Heart to the very heart of God.

Obedience

In the heavenly tapestry of virtues, Mary's obedience stands as a luminous thread, weaving a narrative of profound submission and divine alignment. Her life, a continual "fiat" to the will of God, reveals the profound beauty of an obedient heart. From the moment of the Annunciation, Mary offered herself completely to God, her lips uttering a response that would change the course of history: "Behold the handmaid of the Lord; be it unto me according to thy word."

Obedience, in its truest form, is more than mere compliance. It is an act of love, a surrender to the divine wisdom that surpasses human understanding. In the Blessed Virgin, we see the perfect model of this virtue. She did not question the angel Gabriel's message, nor did she resist the path laid before her, one fraught with unknowns and sufferings. Instead, she embraced it fully, recognizing that obedience to God's will is the pathway to true sanctity and joy.

The theological bedrock of Mary's obedience is rooted in her immaculate heart. Free from the stain of original sin, her will was perfectly aligned with God's will. This purity allowed her to live a life of continual yes, embodying the harmony between human freedom and divine will. She teaches us that obedience is not a restriction but a liberation, unlocking the deepest potentials of our being when we trustfully surrender to God's plan.

Mary's obedience also illuminates the profound relationship between freedom and submission. In our contemporary world, where personal autonomy is often elevated to ultimate importance, her life stands in stark contrast. She showed that true freedom is found not in self-assertion but in self-giving. By saying yes to God, her soul magnified the Lord, and her spirit rejoiced in God her Savior. Her obedience was the gateway to her own exaltation, proving that in losing one's life for God's sake, one truly finds it.

Consider the humble setting of the Nativity. Mary's obedience brought her to Bethlehem, where she gave birth to the Savior in a manger. Her submission to the decrees of the Roman Empire and her acceptance of scanty accommodations for the birth of Christ are profound acts of trust and surrender. She didn't seek comfort or recognition but fulfilled her role in God's salvific plan with meekness and faith.

This virtue of obedience continued throughout her life, reflecting in every moment of her journey with Jesus. From fleeing to Egypt at a moment's notice to protect the infant Jesus to seeking Him anxiously in the temple, Mary continually submitted to God's directions. Her trust in divine providence allowed her to navigate the sorrows and joys of motherhood with unwavering faith.

Moreover, at the wedding feast in Cana, her command to the servants, "Do whatever he tells you," encapsulates her profound understanding of obedience. She recognized Jesus' divine authority and instructed others to follow His guidance. Here, Mary bridges her own obedience to God's will with guiding others toward the same path, showing that her obedience was not passive but actively participatory in God's unfolding plan.

At the foot of the Cross, Mary's obedience reached its pinnacle. Witnessing her Son's crucifixion, she endured immense suffering with serene acceptance. Her silent presence at Calvary testified to her unwavering commitment to God's will, even when it demanded the ultimate sacrifice of her own maternal heart. Through her sorrow, she united herself perfectly to the redemptive mission of Christ, exemplifying how obedience often entails embracing suffering for a greater glory.

Her entire life becomes a testament to what Saint Elizabeth identified during the Visitation, "Blessed is she who believed that what was spoken to her by the Lord would be fulfilled." This statement not only acknowledges her faith but profoundly points to the obedience that undergirded her belief. She didn't just believe passively but actively lived out her faith through obedient action, making her the exemplar of combining faith with works.

In understanding Mary's obedience, we also catch a glimpse of her unique role as the new Eve. Just as Eve's disobedience led to the Fall, Mary's obedience opened the door to redemption. In saying "yes" to God, she became co-operator with grace, echoing the divine fiat that initiated creation. Her obedience becomes a new genesis, a reordering of human will towards divine harmony.

Her life encourages the faithful to cultivate a similar disposition of heart. In a world rife with distraction and dissent, Mary's example beckons us towards surrender and trust in God's providence. By following her model, we learn that obedience is not about losing our identity but about discovering our true selves in God's service.

Thus, in liturgies, prayers, and personal devotions, we often invoke Mary as a model of obedience. She is called "Mother Most Obedient" in various litanies. This title reinforces her readiness to listen and respond to God, drawing believers into a deeper meditative reflection on their own lives. Devotion to Mary's obedience stirs within the Christian heart a desire to conform to God's will, acknowledging that such conformity leads to the fulfillment of divine love in us.

In conclusion, Mary's obedience is not simply a subject of theological admiration but a living call to each one of us. It is a path marked by humility, trust, and an unyielding faith in God's goodness. Following her example, Catholics are invited to say their own "fiat" to God, allowing the Holy Spirit to work through their lives, transforming ordinary moments into acts of divine grace. Mary's obedient heart continues to be a beacon for all who seek the path of holiness, guiding them to the ultimate union with God in love and truth.

Poverty

The Blessed Virgin Mary's embrace of poverty is nothing short of a celestial paradox, a wealth richer than the coffers of kingdoms. She, who bore the King of Kings, chose a path of temporal deprivation, rendering her a captivating paradox of divine grandeur enrobed in humble simplicity.

From the moment of the Annunciation, her acceptance of poverty became evident. This maiden of Nazareth, who found favor with God, responded to the angelic greeting not with a demand for privilege but with an utterance of sublime humility: "Behold the handmaid of the Lord; be it done unto me according to thy word." In this single statement, Mary aligned herself with the divine will, willingly embracing a life devoid of worldly riches.

In the grotto of Bethlehem, her choice manifests vividly. The nativity scene is set not in a palace adorned with gold but in a humble stable, where the simplicity of her surroundings enriches the majesty of the Incarnation. Mary swaddles the Infant Jesus in her arms, offering Him to the shepherds and the Magi. Her poverty here becomes the canvas upon which divine providence paints the first strokes of redemption.

So too, at the Presentation in the Temple, Mary offers a pair of turtledoves, the sacrifice of the poor, as prescribed by Mosaic Law. In her act, we glimpse a heart detached from material wealth, fully anchored in heavenly treasures. This gesture reflects a soul that understands true wealth is not found in the abundance of possessions but in an unwavering faith and love for God.

As we journey farther into the narrative of her life, we see Mary again in Nazareth, living a simple, obscure existence. There, in the home she shared with Joseph and Jesus, she exemplifies the quiet dignity of poverty. Her daily life would have been marked by modesty and industry, her hands busy with the work of the household while her heart remained ever contemplative of divine mysteries.

This commitment to poverty is evident even at the crucifixion, where Mary stands at the foot of the Cross. There, stripped of all earthly comforts, she witnesses her Son's ultimate sacrifice. Her soul, pierced by the sword of sorrow, radiates an extraordinary strength and grace. This profound act of solidarity with Christ embodies her virtue of poverty more poignantly than any dwelling of brick and mortar ever could.

But Mary's poverty is not just a physical condition; it is a spiritual disposition, a voluntary surrender to God's providence. This kind of poverty, affluent in spiritual riches, resonates deeply with the teachings of her Son. Jesus proclaimed, "Blessed are the poor in spirit, for theirs is the kingdom of heaven." Mary, the first and most perfect disciple, internalized this beatitude, making it the anthem of her existence.

In embracing poverty, Mary invites us to understand a hidden but paramount truth: to be poor in spirit is to open oneself to the treasures of divine grace. Her life demonstrates that to relinquish everything is, paradoxically, to gain everything of true and lasting value. She teaches us to rely not on our own strength or material comforts, but on God's infinite mercy and love.

This virtue of poverty positions Mary as the ultimate exemplar for the faithful. Her life, radiating simplicity and inner richness, sets forth a model for those seeking to walk the narrow path of sanctity. To follow her is to view material wealth as transient and to hunger for the eternal grace that comes from total trust in God.

In our own lives, we are constantly faced with choices that test our attachment to worldly goods. Mary, in her quiet yet profound way, shows us how to navigate these decisions. Her example encourages us to cultivate a spirit of poverty, detaching ourselves from material excess and dedicating our lives to the pursuit of spiritual virtue.

Thus, Mary's poverty becomes a guiding star, illuminating the path toward a deeper communion with God. Her life teaches that true freedom is found not in the possession of many things but in the purity of heart that seeks God above all. She stands as a testament to the transformative power of poverty embraced out of love for the Creator.

As we meditate on Mary's life and her virtue of poverty, let us strive to embody this virtue in our own journeys. Like Mary, we are called to trust in God's providence, to find joy in simplicity, and to seek the spiritual riches that can never be taken away. Her example beckons us to a deeper, more authentic discipleship, one that finds its ultimate fulfillment in the embrace of our Heavenly Father.

May the Blessed Virgin Mary, our model of poverty, intercede for us, that we may grow in this virtue and draw closer to the Heart of her Son, Jesus Christ. In following her example, may we come to know the true wealth that lies in the love and grace of God.

Patience

Patience, like a silken thread, weaves its way through the tapestry of the Blessed Virgin Mary's life. Rooted profoundly in her unwavering faith and steadfast love, Mary's patience is both a testament to her divine grace and a guiding light for all who seek to emulate her virtues. In the silent whispers of the Annunciation, in the tender moments at the foot of the Cross, and in the hopeful awaiting of the Resurrection, Mary's patience shines brilliantly.

From the moment the Archangel Gabriel announced God's grand plan for her, Mary embraced the virtue of patience with an open heart. This serene acceptance, devoid of any trace of doubt or haste, reveals her deep trust in God's timing. She knew that the fulfillment of God's promises would unfold in divine rhythm, beyond the grasp of human urgency. This profound patience is a cornerstone of her sanctity, setting her apart as the chosen vessel of God's grace.

Consider the early years of Jesus' life. The Virgin Mother nurtured Him with unending patience, knowing that the seeds of divine mission would take time to grow and flourish. Each moment, each day, was an exercise in quiet anticipation and unwavering trust. As Jesus grew, so did the challenges. Yet, Mary's patience never wavered. Whether in the temple, finding

Jesus among the scholars, or at the wedding feast at Cana, her patient heart remained a constant, guiding force.

And what of the crucifixion? There, amidst the agony and sorrow, Mary's patience reached its zenith. Standing beneath the Cross, her soul pierced by a sword of suffering, she waited, believing that even in death, God's plan was unfolding. Her patience was not passive endurance; it was an active, living faith, a profound surrender to the mysteries of divine providence. It was the patience of a heart that knew joy and sorrow are intertwined threads in the sacred narrative of redemption.

In this way, Mary's patience extends beyond mere forbearance into the realms of theological reflection. It teaches us about the intricate connection between time and eternity. Patience is not just waiting; it is an active engagement with the present moment, a profound trust in God's eternal promises. This wisdom transforms our understanding of life's trials, helping us see them not as obstacles but as opportunities for deeper union with God.

Mary's patience also embodies a metaphysical stillness, an inner tranquility that reflects her intimate communion with the Holy Trinity. This stillness is not the absence of action but the presence of divine peace. It is the calm center within the tempest, a reflection of her Immaculate Heart, undisturbed by the world's chaos. Her patience teaches us to find this stillness within ourselves, to cultivate a heart that listens for God's whisper amidst the clamor of life.

Moreover, the Virgin's patience stands as a bulwark against despair. In a world driven by instant gratification and restless pursuits, Mary's virtue of patience calls us back to the essence of faithful waiting. It is a reminder that God's timeline is not ours, and His plans often unfold in ways that transcend our understanding. This virtue empowers us to endure suffering with grace, to face uncertainties with hope, and to await God's salvation with unwavering confidence.

In our modern lives, Mary's example of patience offers a sanctuary of peace and a beacon of hope. It invites us to slow down, to embrace each moment as a gift, and to trust in the unseen workings of divine grace. Whether we are waiting for a prayer to be answered, a dream to be realized, or a cross to be lifted, Mary's patience inspires us to remain steadfast and serene, knowing that God's love is always at work.

Through the lens of poetic grace and deep theological insight, we see that Mary's patience is not a passive waiting but an active participation in God's redemptive plan. It is a dynamic interweaving of trust, faith, and love, a testament to the spiritual strength found in a heart fully surrendered to God. Her life, marked by patient endurance, calls us to a deeper understanding of this virtue, inviting us to follow her example in our own journeys.

In reflecting on Mary's patience, let us seek to embody this virtue in our own lives. Let us find inspiration in her unwavering faith, draw strength from her serene acceptance, and strive to cultivate a heart that trusts in God's perfect timing. May the Blessed Virgin Mary's example guide us in all our trials, leading us to a deeper union with God through the grace of patient endurance.

Mercy

Mary's mercy is a gentle veil, softly woven through the fabric of her being, every thread imbued with divine compassion. Her mercy is not just an abstract quality, but a living, breathing essence that shapes her very existence. It resounds in the ears of those who seek solace and echoes in the hearts of those who seek forgiveness. Mary, the Mother of Mercy, is a beacon for those lost in the wilderness of despair, an anchor for those adrift in the tempest of their own making.

Through her actions, Mary has demonstrated an immeasurable capacity for mercy. Her willingness to intercede on behalf of sinners, her ceaseless prayers for the redemption of souls, and her tender compassion towards humanity illustrate a mercy that knows no bounds. The stories of her intercessions are countless, each one a testament to her loving nature. She is a channel through which God's mercy flows, an unbreakable bridge between humanity and the divine.

In the quiet town of Cana, we witness Mary's mercy. At a wedding feast where joy could have turned to shame, Mary noticed the plight of the hosts running out of wine. Her intercession with Jesus, her gentle insistence upon His first miracle, exemplifies her merciful heart. She saw a need, felt compassion, and took action. This simple yet profound act holds endless depth, revealing her sensitivity to human needs and her readiness to act in kindness.

Mary's merciful love extends beyond the pages of scripture into the lives of the faithful. Every prayer, every supplication directed to her is met with a heart full of understanding and compassion. In her, we find not only a Mediatrix but also a mother—always listening, always caring. She embraces our sufferings, she consoles our sorrows, and she accompanies us on our journey toward redemption.

The saints often speak of Mary's mercy with deep reverence. St. Alphonsus Liguori, in his writings, beautifully encapsulates this sentiment. He speaks of Mary's merciful nature as a remedy to despair, a comforting presence in the darkest of times. Her mercy is not just a reflection of her own character but a manifestation of God's infinite compassion. Through Mary, we get a glimpse of the divine mercy that awaits us.

Mercy, as embodied by Mary, is never passive or indifferent. It is active, dynamic, and transformative. It's a mercy that prompts action, stimulates change, and fosters growth. To invoke Mary's mercy is to invite a profound change within oneself, a transformation guided by her gentle yet firm hand. Her mercy turns our hearts towards God, encouraging us to seek forgiveness and fostering in us a genuine desire for repentance.

Consider the countless apparitions of Mary throughout history, each one a testament to her merciful concern for humanity. Whether at Lourdes, Fatima, or Guadalupe, Mary's message remains constant—a call to repentance, to prayer, to a deeper relationship with God. It is a mother's plea, tender yet urgent, merciful yet resolute. She seeks not to condemn but to save, not to chastise but to guide.

Mary's mercy is a source of hope for all. In her, we find a refuge from the storms of life, a sanctuary of peace amidst the chaos of the world. Her mercy is a light in the darkness, leading us out of the shadows of our sins into the glorious light of God's love. It is a mercy that heals, restores, and renews. Her intercession brings divine compassion into our lives, offering us the grace to overcome our shortcomings and the strength to walk the path of righteousness.

In our devotion to Mary, we are called to emulate her merciful heart. It is not enough to merely venerate her; we must strive to follow her example. Her life teaches us that mercy is an essential virtue, one that must permeate every aspect of our existence. To be merciful is to be Christ-like, and in Mary, we see the perfect embodiment of this divine mercy.

As priests and faithful, we must teach and preach about Mary's mercy, ensuring that this profound aspect of her character is known and cherished. In our sermons, our teachings, our daily lives, let us reflect this mercy. Let us be channels of her compassion, bringing comfort to the suffering, hope to the despairing, and love to the unloved. In doing so, we honor Mary and propagate devotion to her, spreading her message of mercy far and wide.

In conclusion, Mary's mercy is a cornerstone of her virtues, a divine gift that she shares with the world. It is a luminance that brightens the path to salvation, offering solace, compassion, and love. Through her merciful heart, we find a profound connection to God's boundless mercy. Let us embrace this gift, cherish it, and, like Mary, extend it to all who cross our paths. May her mercy always guide us, uplift us, and lead us ever closer to the heart of God.

Sorrow

The virtue of Sorrow within the Blessed Virgin Mary is not just a singular moment of grief but a profound and continuous outpouring of her immaculate heart. This sorrow is intricately intertwined with her unwavering faith and unbroken devotion. It is not the sorrow of despair but of compassionate love, reflecting the duality of her existence as both a mother and the first disciple of Christ.

From the Annunciation to the crucifixion, Mary's life was touched by a series of poignant sorrows, each one more profound than the last. Her heart grieved at Simeon's prophecy, foretelling the future pangs of motherhood intertwined with the destiny of her Son. "Behold, this child is destined for the fall and rise of many in Israel, and to be a sign that will be contradicted," he declared. Yet Mary, in her humility, accepted the divine will with a heart that resonated with an immense capacity for loving sorrow.

Her sorrow was not a passive acceptance. It was an active participation in the redemption narrative. She stood by the Cross, a testament to faith amidst incomprehensible pain. Those hours at Golgotha were the crucible where her sorrows were most acutely felt, and yet, they became a wellspring of spiritual strength for the ages to come. She, who conceived without sin, also bore the world's pain without murmur.

Mary's sorrow extends beyond personal grief to encompass the collective suffering of humanity. In her numerous apparitions, from Lourdes to Fatima, she comes as a mother deeply aggrieved by the sins of the world. She urges repentance, not from a place of condemnation, but from a sorrowful heart yearning to guide her children back to the path of righteousness.

At the heart of Marian sorrow lies a unique form of mercy. It's a sorrow that sees beyond individual faults to the broader tapestry of human frailty. This is the mourning of a mother who, despite being untainted by sin, understands the full weight of sin's impact. She weeps not for herself but for the souls entrapped in sin's chains, always beckoning them towards redemption and grace.

In a philosophical vein, Mary's sorrow can be said to transcend temporal limitations. It's an eternal echo, reverberating through the corridors of time, a sorrow that both anticipates and remembers. This sorrow is illuminated by divine wisdom, exemplifying a profound understanding of human plight and the mysterious ways of God's providence.

Her sorrow is an invitation to the faithful—to enter into a more intimate communion with her Son, to recognize in their personal sufferings a share in the Cross of Christ. This sorrow is not an end in itself but a pathway to deeper spiritual joy, rooted in the hope of the resurrection. For every tear Mary shed, there is a corresponding grace, a benevolent exchange of divine mercy for human suffering.

Thus, the sorrow of Mary is a spiritual mystery, a luminous sorrow that guides the faithful through their own valleys of tears. It's a sorrow imbued with the light of hope, encouraging believers to embrace their crosses, knowing that the Queen of Sorrows is perpetually interceding on their behalf.

No reflection on the sorrows of Mary would be complete without recognizing the Seven Sorrows—a devotion deeply embedded in Catholic tradition. From the prophecy of Simeon to the burial of her Son, each sorrow holds a mirror to Mary's soul, revealing layers of divine virtue and strength. Her heart, pierced by swords, yet remained steadfast in faith—an icon of perfect sorrow and unyielding hope.

In contemplating her sorrows, the faithful are drawn to appreciate the silent yet profound ways in which Mary's sorrows shaped her earthly journey. She teaches us that true sorrow does not lead to despair but to a closer union with God. Her life is a testament to the redemptive power of sorrow infused with divine love.

Mary's sorrow is like a deep well from which flows endless consolation for the sorrowful. It beckons the weary and the burdened to find refuge in a maternal heart that understands every pain. Her sorrows, sacred and sublime, are a bridge to the divine, offering solace not just to those who mourn, but to all who seek a deeper understanding of God's love.

Let us then, through the contemplation of Mary's sorrows, draw nearer to her loving heart. There, in the depths of her sorrow, we find an impeccable model of virtue and an unparalleled source of divine grace.

Chapter 3: Mary in Sacred Scripture

In the kaleidoscope of Sacred Scripture, the Blessed Virgin Mary emerges as a luminous figure, her presence discernible both in the shadows of the Old Testament and the radiant clarity of the New Testament. A tapestry woven by divine hands, her role is foretold in the prophecies and fulfilled in the Gospels. The locales of Bethlehem, Nazareth, and Calvary become sacred theatres where the silent symphony of Mary's life unfolds, a narrative suffused with divine obsequies and human pathos. Within these hallowed texts, one perceives a constellation of virtues: her unwavering obedience to God's will, her profound humility, and her impenetrable faith, forming a celestial guide for all who seek to draw closer to the heart of Christ through his Mother. As theology and history converge, Mary stands as both the Ark of the Covenant and the New Eve, harmonizing the Old and New Testaments with her Fiat, her willing 'Yes' to God, embodying both prophetic anticipation and divine fulfillment.

Old Testament Foreshadowing

Within the hallowed passages of the Old Testament, the Blessed Virgin Mary reveals herself through allegories, symbols, and prophetic verses. Like the dawn before the radiant sun, she predates her grand New Testament appearance, veiled but evident to those with eyes of faith and hearts attuned to divine mysteries. Just as the Ark of the Covenant encapsulated the very essence of God's promise to His people, so too would Mary, in the fullness of time, carry within her the Word made Flesh.

The Ark of the Covenant, crafted under divine instruction by Bezaleel, was pure and immaculate in its construction. Overlaid with gold, it held the Tablets of the Law, Aaron's rod that budded, and a pot of manna—all foreshadowing elements of Mary. She became the living Ark, her purity untarnished and her soul a vibrant testament to God's restorative grace. Her unstained nature made her a fitting vessel for Christ, the Bread of Life, and High Priest in the order of Melchizedek.

Consider, also, the poetic hymns of the Psalms, especially the psalm that speaks of the queen arrayed in gold at the right hand of the King (Psalm 45:9). Is this not a glimpse of Mary, the Queen of Heaven, who stands beside her Son, the eternal King? David, in his inspired poetry, sings not only of earthly majesties but unfolds a vision of the heavenly splendor, pointing us toward the Virgin Mary and her regal dignity.

Moreover, Isaiah's prophecies shed transcendent light upon the coming of the Virgin. Isaiah 7:14 proclaims, "Behold, a virgin shall conceive, and bear a son, and shall call his name Immanuel." This is no mere coincidence or abstract prophecy. This is a celestial blueprint laid down by God's own hand, manifesting in Mary's humble "fiat." Through her, Emmanuel indeed comes to dwell among us, God incarnate through the vessel of a virgin, pure and full of grace.

The Book of Genesis, too, intricately interweaves Mary's prefiguration in its sacred narrative. In Genesis 3:15, we witness the Protoevangelium, or the first gospel, where God declares that the woman's seed will crush the serpent's head. This enigmatic woman is none other than Mary, whose divine maternity brings forth the salvation of mankind through Jesus Christ. Here lies the profound mystery of Mary's role in God's redemptive plan, conceived in God's mind from the beginning, infused with the promise of ultimate victory over sin and death.

Further, consider the poetic imagery found in the Song of Songs. While an evocative and mysterious text, its layers conceal a depth of Marian significance. The Bride, often interpreted as Israel or the Church, can also be seen as a type of Mary. "Thou art all fair, my love; there is no spot in thee" (Song of Songs 4:7). In these words, we detect a delicate whisper of the Immaculate Conception, a prefiguration bearing witness to Mary's all-encompassing beauty and purity, untouched by original sin.

Sail through the deep waters of the Old Testament, and you discover more shadows foretelling Mary. In Judith and Esther, we encounter prefigurations of Mary's unique role in salvation history. Judith, whose courageous act delivers Israel from Holofernes, and Esther, who risks her life to save her people, both point to Mary. In her obedience and humility, Mary becomes the ultimate heroine who, by giving birth to the Savior, liberates humanity from the bondage of sin.

In the person of Ruth, Mary is foreshadowed in her loyalty, fidelity, and humble acceptance of a divine plan. Ruth's union with Boaz, leading to the birth of Obed, grandfather of David, paves the way for Christ's lineage. In Ruth's story, we reflect upon Mary's "yes" to God, which ushers in the Divine Savior, fulfilling the promise made to David – that his throne shall endure forever through Christ.

We turn our gaze to wisdom literature, where the virtues extolled mirror the virtues of our Blessed Mother. Proverbs 31 describes the "woman of valor," whose worth is far beyond jewels. Her wisdom, diligence, and maternally nurturing spirit anticipate

Mary's role as the Mother of God, whose exquisite virtues shine luminously in the eyes of the faithful. In these sentiments, the Scriptures wrap Mary's radiance in words that continue to inspire and elevate the faithful's devotion to her.

Thus, through the canvas of the Old Testament, from its genesis to its flourishing, we discern the delicate brushstrokes that anticipate the glorious figure of Mary. These foreshadowings enrich our understanding and deepen our reverence, compelling us to recognize the divine symphony of salvation history. Each symbol and prophecy draws us nearer to the ineffable mystery of the Virgin Most Holy, forming a sacred mosaic that heralds her destined role in God's salvific plan.

As we delve into these sacred texts, it is with a heart of devotion and eyes opened to the sublime intersections of prophecy and fulfillment. The Old Testament not only prepares the way for the Incarnation but does so enfolded in the maternal foreshadowing of Mary's sublime and predestined part in the divine narrative. Her presence, concealed yet manifold, manifests a prototypical glimpse of the grace and glory that will fully blossom in the New Testament.

It is an invitation, then, to approach these texts anew, to peer beyond the veil, and to encounter Mary in the whispers of ancient promises and the shadows of divine foreshadowing. It is an invitation to magnify our reverence for her, who shines as the preeminent fulfillment of God's loving covenant with humanity.

New Testament Fulfillment

In the delicate and resplendent tapestry of Sacred Scripture, the Blessed Virgin Mary occupies a position of profound and unique significance. The full splendor of her role unfolds in the New Testament, symbolizing the perfect unity of divine promise and its consummation. As the dawn of salvation manifests through Christ, Mary stands as the immaculate portal through which God's grace enters humanity. This juxtaposition of divine and human elements introduces not just the fulfillment of an ancient covenant, but also the emergence of eternal hope.

The scenes of the Annunciation and the Magnificat paint a picture of unparalleled grace. When the Archangel Gabriel appeared to Mary with the divine message, her acceptance, simple yet profound, reverberated through the celestial realms. "Behold the handmaid of the Lord; be it unto me according to thy word" (*Luke 1:38*). This moment, imbued with humility and obedience, signifies humanity's acquiescence to the divine will. Through her, the eternal Word became flesh, transforming the temporal sphere into a vessel of divine love and the infinite.

Mary's role is not limited to passive acceptance but extends to active participation in the mystery of salvation. At the wedding feast in Cana, she intercedes with a silent yet potent authority. "They have no wine" (*John 2:3*), she informs her Son, eliciting His first public miracle. Her intercession here unravels the inherent depth of her maternal role, embodying both compassion and foresight. She foreshadows her perpetual mission as Mediatrix, one who continually intercedes for humanity.

At the foot of the Cross, Mary's maternal suffering reaches its climax in divine solidarity. Here, she becomes Co-Redemptrix, sharing in the sacrifice of her Son. Her soul, prophesied by Simeon to be pierced by a sword (*Luke 2:35*), bears the sorrow of the world's redemption. This heartbreak of a mother, interwoven with the divine sorrow of the Son, encapsulates the divine plan's fulfillment, binding the human and divine in a mystical union of suffering and grace.

One cannot overlook the poignant scene where Jesus, from the Cross, entrusts Mary to John, saying, "Woman, behold your son" and to the disciple, "Behold your mother" (*John 19:26-27*). This testament brings to fruition the communal and ecclesiastical dimension of Mary's role. It signifies Mary's adoption as the spiritual mother of all believers, encompassing all humanity in her maternal embrace. The nascent Church finds its first spiritual anchor in the person of Mary, who, through her unwavering faith, becomes a model for all disciples.

The Acts of the Apostles introduces us to Mary in her role in the early Church. Here, she is found in the upper room, praying with the Apostles, dwellers of the nascent Church, awaiting the promised Holy Spirit (*Acts 1:14*). Her presence underscores her continual role as a source of strength and unity for the early believers. It is through her, in communion with the Holy Spirit, that the Church finds its nurturing and maternal heart.

Mary's magnificence lies not just in the moments of divine revelation and miraculous wonders, but also in her ordinary, daily acts of faith and love. Her silent meditations, her tender care, and her silent yet steadfast companionship with her Son provide a compelling illustration of living a life in total alignment with God's will. Mary's assumed presence throughout her Son's ministry and the edifying support she offers accentuate her active and continuous collaboration in the divine mission.

The Apostle John's Revelation offers yet another glimpse of the exaltation of Mary in the apocalyptic vision. The "woman clothed with the sun, with the moon under her feet, and a crown of twelve stars on her head" (*Revelation 12:1*) stands as an eternal symbol of her queenship and immaculate purity. This vision, rich with symbolic meaning, underscores her perpetual victory over evil and her coronation as the Queen of Heaven, encapsulating the Church victorious.

In Mary, we find the perfect harmonization of the finite and infinite, a living testament to God's extraordinary grace operating within the realm of the ordinary. Her life serves as a luminous example that devotion is both an ascent into the divine and a descent into the service of humankind. More than just the biological mother of Jesus, she becomes an emblem of perfect discipleship, a beacon guiding us to deeper union with Christ.

Verily, the New Testament allows us to witness the assured fulfillment of Old Testament prophecies and the inauguration of a new covenant through Mary. Her fiat is not just an assent but a lifelong symphony of divine cooperation. Through her, we see the unfolding of God's salvific plan, drawing every heart into the immaculate and infinite love of the Creator through the Savior's beckoning.

Mary's fulfillment of divine prophecy, thus, transcends the mere chronological events of her life. It represents the timeless and unending invitation to enter the divine mystery through faith and devotion. This invitation perpetually resonates with generations of believers, fostering an unbroken chain of spiritual heritage centered on her virtues and maternal care.

Chapter 4: Mary in Sacred Tradition

To trace the steps of Mary through the sacred corridors of Tradition is to wade into a river that buoys us on currents of holy reverence and profound affection. The early Church Fathers, imbued with the luminous grace of divine wisdom, spoke of Mary not simply as a figure of history but as an eternal beacon guiding the faithful. From the catacombs where the first Christians whispered prayers to her, to the grand basilicas where her name resounds in chants that ascend to the heavens, Marian devotion has blossomed through the ages. With each century, new layers of veneration emerged, enfolding her in ever-deeper hues of theological insight and heartfelt worship. She stands, radiant and inviolate, a serene Madonna above the troubled seas of human endeavor, her presence a steadfast testament to the Church's enduring love and unwavering trust in her maternal intercession. This hallowed tradition forms an unbroken chain, linking the fervent hearts of believers across millennia, and in this sacred lineage, Mary's role remains not merely significant but utterly sanctifying.

Early Church Fathers

In the splendid mosaic of Marian devotion, the voices of the
Early Church Fathers resonate with a singularly profound timbre.
Their writings, suffused with reverence and theological insight,
form a bedrock upon which the edifice of Marian veneration
stands firm. Indeed, the Early Church Fathers not only defended
the nascent Christian faith but also laid the groundwork for our
deep-seated love and theological understanding of the Blessed
Virgin Mary.

The Church Fathers saw in Mary a mirror reflecting the divine.
Their words, like shining beacons, illuminate the path for the
faithful who seek to understand more deeply the mysteries of
Mary. Take, for instance, St. Ignatius of Antioch. In his letters,
he exalts Mary as the one who nurtures the Savior in her womb, a
temple wherein the divine and the human perpetually commune.
His words awaken in us a profound sense of Mary's role in the
Incarnation, urging us to honor her with the utmost devotion.

Consider also St. Irenaeus of Lyons. In his writings, Mary is cast
as the New Eve, a figure of redemption and grace. Whereas Eve's
disobedience brought forth the fall of man, Mary's fiat—her
obedient "Yes"—opened the doors to salvation. Her willingness
to partake in God's divine plan positioned her not just as a
passive vessel but as an active participant in mankind's

redemption. It is as though each time we pray the "Hail Mary," we echo the sentiments first explored by Irenaeus, reaffirming our belief in Mary's pivotal role in the divine economy.

In the Eastern tradition, St. Cyril of Alexandria stands as a luminous figure in Marian theology. Not content with acknowledging Mary merely as the Mother of Jesus, Cyril insists on her title as Theotokos—the God-bearer. In doing so, he safeguards the doctrine of the Incarnation, affirming that Jesus is both fully human and fully divine, a truth brought forth in the sanctified space of Mary's womb. Cyril's defense of Mary as Theotokos at the Council of Ephesus reverberates through the ages, compelling us to approach her not merely as a historical figure but as the Mother of God, forever worthy of our veneration.

St. Ambrose of Milan, who stands as a pillar of Western Christianity, offers a meditation on Mary's virtues. For Ambrose, Mary epitomizes virginity, humility, and obedience. Through Mary, Ambrose teaches the faithful how to embody these virtues in their own lives. His exhortations on Marian devotion are not mere theological musings; they are practical pathways to holiness, revealing how an authentic Marian devotion inexorably leads us closer to Christ.

St. Augustine of Hippo, known for his profound theological insights, also contributes richly to Marian thought. He sees Mary as the Mother of the Church, a guiding star in the tumultuous seas of human existence. Augustine's reflections emphasize the transformative power of grace, of which Mary is both the recipient and the dispenser. For him, devotion to Mary is a logical extension of understanding Christ's redemptive work, thus inviting us into a deeper relationship with our Lord through His most Holy Mother.

Now consider the thoughts of St. John Chrysostom. Known as "Golden Mouth" for his eloquence, he likewise extols Mary, meshing poetic grandeur with spiritual truths. His homilies penetrate the veil separating heaven and earth, depicting Mary as an intercessor of unparalleled efficacy. His vivid imagery and emotive language paint Mary not as an inaccessible celestial queen but as a loving mother interceding for her children. Each word is an invitation to approach her with confidence, trusting in her maternal care.

Origen of Alexandria, an early theologian and philosopher, offers contemplative depth. He digs into the ancient prophecies and types, seeing Mary prefigured in the Old Testament. Origen likens her to the Burning Bush that burns but is not consumed, a fitting metaphor for her perpetual virginity and her purity illuminated by divine light. This spiritual, almost mystic interpretation brings a richness to Marian devotion, encouraging us to see her as a living fulfillment of ancient prophecies.

In the fertile soil of Patristic thought, we also find Tertullian who contrasts Mary's obedience with Eve's disobedience, a theme echoed throughout patristic literature. For Tertullian, Mary's "Yes" is not a simple act but a cosmic event that realigns the very fabric of humanity's relationship with the Creator. Each act of veneration toward Mary is, in a sense, participation in this cosmic realignment.

As we traverse this sacred narrative, the legacy of the Early Church Fathers beckons us into deeper waters of faith. Their theological musings are not relics of antiquity but vibrant, living testimonies that urge us to elevate our own devotion to Mary. In their reflections, we find a call to action, an invitation to let Marian devotion permeate every aspect of our Christian lives.

The Early Church Fathers' insights form a symphony, a harmonious blend of theology, philosophy, and mysticism, all dedicated to exalting the Blessed Virgin Mary. Their collective wisdom and spiritual depth beckon us through the corridors of time, urging us to honor Mary, not merely as a historical figure, but as our eternal Mother, our advocate, and the mirror of divine grace. Their teachings elevate our understanding, transform our veneration, and guide us on the path to deeper union with Christ.

Marian Devotion Through the Ages

From the very first days of the Church, Marian devotion has blossomed as a fragrant garden nurtured by the waters of grace and light of true faith. Across centuries, this devotion, initially tender and filled with awe, has grown to touch the highest peaks of mysticism and the broadest plains of communal worship. Each era, a unique mosaic of culture and faith, has unearthed new facets of the radiant gem that is Mary's place in our spiritual life.

In the early centuries, the seeds of Marian devotion took root amidst the fertile minds of the early Church Fathers. Luminaries like St. Irenaeus and St. Justin Martyr recognized Mary as the New Eve, whose obedience and faithfulness reversed the curse of the first. Their theological ruminations were not merely academic exercises; they were profound affirmations of Mary's singular role in the divine plan of salvation. These roots grew deep, finding nourishment in the reverent hearts of the faithful, who flocked to Marian shrines and celebrated her feasts with solemn adoration.

The Middle Ages saw a blossoming of Marian devotion that painted the sky with the colors of chivalric love and scholastic rigor. St. Bernard of Clairvaux and St. Dominic were among the eminent voices singing the hymns of Mary's unfathomable virtues and her unparalleled intercession. The period was also marked by the construction of magnificent cathedrals, with Notre-Dame as the crowning jewel, where the faithful could gaze upon the splendor of Mary through stained glass windows and statues, lifting their souls to the heavens. This era also gifted the Church with the first meditations on the Rosary, a devotion that would later become a cornerstone of Marian spirituality.

During the Renaissance, the tapestry of Marian devotion was woven with threads of artistic and intellectual prowess. Artists like Michelangelo and Raphael captured the beauty and purity of the Blessed Virgin on canvas, translating theological truths into visual poetry. At the same time, theologians like St. John of the Cross and St. Teresa of Ávila delved into the mystical depths of Marian contemplation, their writings illuminating the way for future generations to seek Mary as the surest path to Christ. This period was both a feast for the eyes and a banquet for the soul, where all senses were invited to partake in the veneration of our Holy Mother.

The Age of Enlightenment, with its emphasis on reason and skepticism, posed a challenge to traditional forms of worship, but even in this era, Marian devotion did not wane. Amidst the rationalist discourse, hearts that sought the comfort and assurance of maternal love turned to Mary. Apparitions such as those at Lourdes and Fatima happened during these times, serving as divine interventions that reaffirmed and revitalized

Marian devotion. These heavenly visitations were not mere spectacles but profound calls to repentance, prayer, and conversion, offering a lighthouse in the stormy seas of skepticism and secularism.

In modern times, Marian devotion has continued to be a vibrant and integral aspect of Catholic life, resonating across all continents and cultures. The Second Vatican Council's document "Lumen Gentium" emphasized Mary's place within the mystery of Christ and the Church, calling for a renewed understanding and veneration of her role. This period saw the emergence of Marian movements, like the Legion of Mary and Schoenstatt Apostolic Movement, which spread the Marian message to every corner of the globe. With each Hail Mary uttered, the faithful draw closer to the Immaculate Heart, finding solace and strength for the trials of contemporary life.

The digital age, with its global connectivity, has also witnessed a unique expression of Marian devotion. Social media, podcasts, and online communities have become new parishes where the love for Mary is shared and celebrated. Pilgrimages to Holy Marian sites can now be attended virtually by those who, for various reasons, can't physically participate. Moreover, the universal language of the internet has made it possible for Marian prayers and devotions to reach millions instantaneously, proving that even in our rapidly changing world, Mary's eternal love remains a constant anchor.

One cannot overlook the influence of the Marian popes, particularly Pope St. John Paul II, whose motto "Totus Tuus" epitomized his total devotion to Mary. His encyclical "Redemptoris Mater" and his establishment of World Youth Days, where millions of young hearts consecrated themselves to the Blessed Mother, have left an indelible mark on the landscape of modern Marian devotion. His pontificate was a beacon, guiding the Church to a deeper, more personal relationship with Mary.

Each epoch in the history of Marian devotion is like a note in a symphony, contributing to a majestic crescendo that sings of Mary's glory and draws the faithful closer to her Immaculate Heart. The melodies of ancient hymns blend seamlessly with modern prayers, creating a timeless echo that reverberates in the hearts of believers. As we move further into the 21st century, the essence of Marian devotion continues to flourish, adapting yet remaining anchored in the eternal truths of the faith.

The pilgrimages, the artistic masterpieces, the theological treatises, all serve as various expressions of one profound truth: Mary is our Mother, ever guiding us to her Son. Each era's unique contribution to Marian devotion reflects the ever-new and ancient love that Mary's presence invokes. In times of peace or turmoil, prosperity or adversity, the faithful have turned their eyes to Mary, finding in her a steadfast intercessor and a model of virtue.

The beautiful tapestry of Marian devotion, woven through the ages, continues to extend its threads, inviting new generations to add their own stitches of love and reverence. With every Ave Maria, whispered in solitude or proclaimed in community, another thread is added, and the centuries-old tradition of honoring Mary grows ever richer. Guided by her gentle hand, the journey of Marian devotion indeed spans time and space, uniting the Church in a unending hymn of praise to the Queen of Heaven.

Chapter 5: Theological Perspectives on Mary

As we delve into the depths of theological reflections on Mary, we encounter a tapestry woven with divine mysteries and spiritual illuminations, beckoning us to contemplate her unparalleled role in the grand symphony of salvation. Mary stands as the archetype of human cooperation with divine grace, her fiat resonating through eternity as a beacon of perfect obedience and love. She is not merely a vessel but the New Eve, whose immaculate purity and unwavering faith configure her intimately with the redemptive mission of Christ. Through her, the Word became flesh, bridging the chasm between the Creator and creation. The theological vistas open to us in studying Mary's role are vast, revealing her as the sublime Mediatrix whose maternal intercession continues to draw souls nearer to her Son. Her place in salvation history is not an appendix but a core doctrine that elevates the understanding of divine mercy and justice. Toward this sacred goal of appreciating Mary's theological significance, our hearts and minds are invited to align with the heavenly harmonies that declare her blessed among women.

Mariology

The essence of Mariology lies within the heart of the Church as it seeks to contemplate and understand the role of the Blessed Virgin Mary in the divine plan of salvation. This theological discipline, swimming in the depths of mystery and grace, extends an invitation to each faithful soul to behold Mary not just as the Mother of Jesus, but as a symbol of pure faith, unyielding hope, and perfect love.

Gazing upon her life, we see a celestial tapestry woven with threads of divine humility and sanctity. From the moment of her immaculate conception, Mary was set apart, sanctified to play an integral role in the salvific mission of her Son. She stands as a singular marvel of creation, crafted by the hand of God to be the New Eve, bearing the Almighty's love in her heart and the Savior in her womb.

In Mariology, we find a reflection of the divine fairness, a mirroring of divine justice and mercy. This isn't merely an academic field but rather a pathway of devotion and veneration. Mary, in her very being, exemplifies the intersection of human and divine. Through her "fiat" — her unwavering assent to God's will — she becomes a vessel of grace, a beacon of divine light illuminating the path toward the Eternal.

The depth of Mariology reveals itself in the myriad ways Mary participates in Christ's redemptive work. To understand Mary is to delve into the great mysteries of the Incarnation and the Paschal Mystery. As Theotokos, the God-bearer, she not only gave birth to Jesus but also nurtured the mystery of the divine in the entirety of her life.

Her humble acceptance, her obedience even unto sorrow, her intimate cooperation with divine grace – all these are not mere historical facts but living testimonies that echo through eternity. They are resonant chords in the symphony of salvation, calling every generation to a higher understanding of divine love.

Mariology also invites us into the shadowy paradox of her sorrow and her joy. This theological pursuit lays bare the sevenfold sorrows that pierced her heart, paralleling the birth pangs of a new creation. The sword that Simeon prophesied became a fulfillment of divine purpose as she stood beneath the cross, her soul entwined with her Son's sacrificial love.

Yet, in her sorrows, there is also an unfathomable joy — the joy of the Resurrection, the joy of her Assumption, the joy of her Coronation as Queen of Heaven. Each dogma related to Mary bends towards capturing this paradox — imbued with divine mystery and human experience. Each dogma lifts the veil slightly on the profundity of Mary's role in God's salvific design.

The virtue of Mary's life offers a mirror for the faithful to behold and strive toward. What does it mean to carry divine grace within? What does it mean to say "yes" unconditionally? Through Mariology, we uncover the beauty of a soul wholly surrendered to God's will, the zenith of sanctified humanity, forever echoing the Magnificat.

Her intercessory power, her role as Mediatrix, and the plethora of titles bestowed upon her by centuries of faithful devotion and theological reflection — all point to a singular realization. Mary is the nexus where heaven meets earth, where the ineffable divine touches the finite human, transforming it. Her soul magnifies the Lord, making His presence known and felt in the most profound ways.

Exploring Mariology isn't just about understanding Marian doctrines; it's about absorbing the very ethos of her existence, letting the purity and simplicity of her faith infuse our own. As we meditate on her virtues, as we delve into the significance of her place in salvation history, we are called to transform, to emulate, to draw closer to the divine through her example.

Through the prism of Mariology, we behold Mary in her multi-faceted roles: not merely the Mother of God but our mother too. Her maternal intercession is a constant source of solace and strength, an unfailing aid in our spiritual journey. She covers us with her mantle, leads us by the hand, and intercedes for us before the throne of grace.

In the sacred journey of Mariology, we are guided by the Church, whose wisdom accumulated over centuries anchors our understanding. The early Church Fathers, with their profound insights, and the continuous thread of Marian devotion stretching through the ages, provide a rich tapestry to explore. The wisdom passed down through tradition is not static but an ever-flowing river of grace that carries us closer to Mary and, through her, to Christ.

Finally, in Mariology, there is an inescapable invitation: to not merely know of Mary, but to know her. It is an invitation to deeper devotion, to heartfelt prayer, and to a more intimate relationship with our Heavenly Mother. The Queen of Heaven beckons us to rise above our earthly limitations, to soar on the wings of faith, hope, and love, towards the brilliant dawn of the glorified Christ she so perfectly embodies.

Thus, Mariology becomes a living, breathing theology. It is the ongoing revelation of the beauty and majesty of the Virgin Mary, inviting the faithful into the mystery of divine intimacy. Her life, her virtues, and her unwavering 'yes' to God continue to illuminate our path, guiding us ever closer to the heart of her Son.

Mary's Role in Salvation History

In the grand tapestry of salvation, Mary shines as an iridescent thread woven with divine intent, shimmering with the brilliance of God's unconditional love. Far beyond a mere passive participant, Mary's role encompasses both profound theological significance and deep, mystical resonance. The grace that God bestowed upon her from her Immaculate Conception, set her apart for a divine mission unparalleled by any other human being.

Contemplating Mary's role in salvation history is akin to diving into an ocean of divine mysteries. Here, we find ourselves enveloped by the waves of grace, each more profound than the last. From the moment of her fiat, when she wholeheartedly accepted God's plan, to her presence at the foot of the Cross, every act and moment of Mary's life became an essential piece in the divine salvific plan. In saying "Yes" to the Incarnation, she opened the gates of Heaven to humanity.

Mary's yes, her fiat, stands as a luminous beacon in the annals of salvation. "Behold, I am the handmaid of the Lord; let it be to me according to your word" (Luke 1:38). This simple yet profound acquiescence changed the course of history. Through her willing cooperation with God's grace, the Word became flesh in her womb. In this divine exchange, Mary became Theotokos, the

God-bearer, encapsulating the mystery of God's transcendence and immanence.

Centuries of theology and devotion have delved into the profound depths of Mary's divine maternity, exploring how this singular event encompasses the essence of God's plan for redemption. At the heart of it all is the Holy Spirit, the Divine Spouse of Mary, covering her with the shadow of the Almighty and bringing forth the Savior, the Light of the World. It is in this ineffable union that human nature was elevated, allowing the grace of salvation to flow abundantly through Mary to the entire world.

Her pivotal role does not end with the birth of Christ. From cradle to Calvary, Mary's presence is unwavering. She nurtures the infant Jesus, educates the boy growing in wisdom and favor, and stands beside Him through His public ministry. At the wedding at Cana, her intercessory power is subtly yet powerfully revealed. "They have no wine," she tells Jesus, setting the stage for His first miracle (John 2:3). In this act, Mary not only unveils Christ's divine mission but also prefigures her future role as mediator and advocate for God's people.

Mary's role reaches its poignant climax at Golgotha, where the prophecy of Simeon that "a sword will pierce through your own soul also" finds its fulfillment (Luke 2:35). Here, the sorrowful mother stands beneath the Cross, embodying the perfect disciple, sharing in Jesus' suffering. Her presence there is not passive; it is active participation in the redemptive suffering of her Son. When Jesus says to John, "Behold, your mother!" and to Mary, "Woman, behold, your son!" (John 19:26-27), He establishes Mary as the spiritual mother of all believers, thus extending her maternal care to the entire Church.

The mystery of Mary's Assumption into Heaven further elevates her role, signifying the ultimate fulfillment of God's promise of salvation to those who are faithful. It is the completion of her earthly journey marked by divine love and obedience. Assumed body and soul into heavenly glory, Mary becomes the eschatological icon of the Church, the sign of hope and comfort to the pilgrim People of God. Her glorified presence in Heaven assures us of the destiny that awaits all who, like her, respond faithfully to God's call.

Throughout the ages, the Church has reflected on Mary's role, deepening its understanding and articulating doctrines that honor her unique participation in God's plan. Titles such as Mediatrix and Co-Redemptrix express these theological truths. As Mediatrix of all graces, Mary is seen as the channel through which the graces of Christ flow to humanity. Her role as Co-Redemptrix emphasizes her unique cooperation in the redemption, a partnership that respects the singular sacrifice of Christ yet acknowledges Mary's indispensable participation.

These titles, while sometimes controversial or misunderstood, seek to capture the profound mystery of Mary's collaboration with the divine. They do not place her on equal footing with Christ but highlight her unique role as the New Eve, whose obedience and faith stand in stark contrast to the disobedience of the first Eve. In juxtaposing Mary's humility with Eve's pride, the Church emphasizes the transformative power of Mary's "Yes," which reverses the curse of sin and death brought into the world through disobedience.

The reverence given to Mary in the liturgy and devotion of the Church reflects her exalted role in salvation history. From the earliest days of Christianity, the faithful have venerated Mary, seeking her intercession and looking to her as a model of pure discipleship. The Marian feasts, hymns, and prayers are not mere acts of devotional excess but profound expressions of theological truths that have sustained the Church throughout the centuries.

Mary, in her humility and obedience, becomes the exemplar for every Christian, showing that true greatness is found in surrendering to God's will. Her life is a testament to the transformative power of grace, demonstrating that human freedom finds its true fulfillment in cooperation with divine providence. As we contemplate her role in salvation history, we are drawn into the mystery of God's love, a love that seeks to elevate and sanctify, to transform and redeem.

In Mary, we see the fullness of what it means to be human, fully receptive to God's grace and fully active in living out that grace. Her maternal care continues from her heavenly throne, where she intercedes for us, her children. To honor Mary is to honor the One who, in His infinite wisdom and love, chose her to be the mother of His Son and the mother of us all. Through Mary, we are invited to receive the grace of Christ more fully, to participate in His redemptive work, and to await with hope the ultimate fulfillment of all God's promises.

Mary's role in salvation history is a rich and multifaceted mystery, inviting us to enter more deeply into the heart of God's salvific plan. As we journey through our own lives, we look to Mary as a constant guide, an intercessor, and a mother who leads us ever closer to her Son, Jesus Christ. In her immaculate being, we find the perfect mirror of divine love, a love that calls us to become, like her, vessels of grace in a world in desperate need of salvation.

Chapter 6: Philosophical Reflections on Marian Virtues

In the vast tapestry of our faith, the virtues of Mary stand as luminous threads woven by the Divine Weaver. To meditate on these virtues is to glimpse into the ethereal harmony between God's grace and human will, an exquisite symphony of purity and strength. Each virtue—purity, humility, fidelity—manifests as a radiant beacon, guiding us toward a life of sanctity. We find in Mary a vessel of divine wisdom and fortitude, embodying both the softness of a mother's touch and the unwavering courage of a spiritual warrior. Her life offers a philosophical paradigm, where the terrestrial and celestial meet in a sublime union, inviting us to perceive our own spiritual journey through the lens of her immaculate heart. Thus, Marian virtues are a profound invitation to align our lives with the eternal, transcendent truths, echoing the call to holiness that whispers through the ages.

Wisdom and Understanding

The virtues of Mary are timeless, an endlessly rich tapestry woven from the threads of her profound wisdom and deep understanding. These two virtues, often spoken of in tandem, are not merely intertwined—they are the very fabric of Marian grace. In contemplating Mary's wisdom and understanding, we enter a celestial realm where logic and love coexist in harmony, inspiring us to seek a higher plane of being and thought.

Wisdom, in the Marian context, transcends mere intellectual prowess. It is an eternal flame, a divine gift that illuminates not just the intellect but the soul. Mary's wisdom is a chorus of heavenly voices guiding her decisions and actions, harmonizing with God's will. She embodies the scriptural pronouncement in Proverbs: "For wisdom is better than rubies; and all the things that may be desired are not to be compared to it." Her wisdom is not an earned accolade but a sacred trust, a divine endowment that surpasses the limitations of human understanding.

Mary's wisdom is most elegantly displayed in her responses to life's profound mysteries. When the angel Gabriel announced that she was chosen to bear the Savior, her affirmation—"Be it unto me according to thy word"—was not born from naivety but from a profound wisdom that recognized divine truth. This wisdom is best understood as a penetrative insight into the eternal truths, a capacity to see beyond the veil of earthly appearances to the divine reality.

As for understanding, it is the inseparable companion of wisdom. Understanding in the Marian sense is the art of compassionate comprehension and empathetic insight. It is a gift from the Holy Spirit that allows Mary to grasp the true essence of events, people, and divine will. Her understanding does not stop at mere knowledge; it penetrates to the heart of divine mysteries, offering solace and insight to those who seek her intercession.

Consider the scene at the Wedding at Cana. Mary's deep understanding of human need and divine timing manifests in her gentle yet compelling directive to Jesus: "They have no wine." Her words, simple yet profound, reveal a wisdom that recognizes not just a lack but also the solution, pointing to Jesus as the source of all fulfillment. Her understanding becomes an avenue for divine grace to act, transforming water into wine, scarcity into abundance.

Through wisdom, Mary discerns the divine will; through understanding, she embraces it with a mother's heart. Her wisdom and understanding are not static virtues but dynamic, ever-responding to the needs and groans of humanity. They call us to a higher standard of life, a life rooted in divine will and overflowing with empathy and spiritual insight.

In the Pietà, we see the culmination of Marian wisdom and understanding. As she cradles the lifeless body of her Son, her eyes are filled not just with sorrow but with a wisdom that sees beyond the agony of the moment to the glory of the resurrection. It is an understanding that encompasses the entirety of salvation history, recognizing the profound significance of Christ's sacrifice. Mary's wisdom and understanding make her the perfect intermediary, the most compassionate Mother who knows the depths of human suffering and the heights of divine glory.

Meditating on Mary's wisdom calls us to cultivate a humble receptivity to divine revelation. It reminds us that true wisdom is not pretentious or self-aggrandizing but quietly transformative. Her understanding invites us to deepen our empathy, to seek to comprehend rather than judge, and to embrace the divine mysteries that unfold in our own lives.

To honor Mary's wisdom and understanding is to acknowledge the divine gifts bestowed upon her and to seek to emulate these virtues in our own lives. We are called to listen more deeply, to discern with greater clarity, and to love with an empathetic heart. Just as Solomon sought wisdom above all treasures, let us too seek the wisdom that comes from above, manifested so perfectly in Mary.

In our veneration of Mary's wisdom and understanding, we are invited to a profound spiritual intimacy with her. She, in her wisdom, guides us; in her understanding, she comforts us. Both virtues serve as a beacon leading us closer to her Son, Jesus Christ. And in our pursuit of these virtues, we come nearer to the heart of God, enveloped in the maternal embrace of Mary Most Holy, the Seat of Wisdom and the Mother of Understanding.

Courage and Fortitude

In the tapestry of Marian virtues, courage and fortitude blaze like bright stars against the night sky, illuminating the path of spiritual resilience for the faithful. The Blessed Virgin Mary, adorned with celestial strength, serves as an emblem of unwavering courage and fortitude. Her life, narrated in the sacred scriptures and hallowed traditions, stands as an everlasting testimony to these virtues, which ought to inspire Roman Catholics and priests in their own journeys of faith.

Consider the Annunciation: when the angel Gabriel appeared and revealed God's divine plan for her, Mary exemplified profound courage. In accepting the mission to be the Mother of the Savior, she opened herself to immense social and personal risk. She faced the potential for public shame and even the prospect of death under the law of her time. Nevertheless, her response, "Behold the handmaid of the Lord; be it unto me according to thy word," quietly echoes the resolve of a soul fortified by divine bravery. Mary's courage was not born of rashness; it sprang from her deep faith and trust in God's providence.

Her fortitude is also poignantly manifested at the foot of the Cross. As Mary witnessed the suffering and crucifixion of her beloved Son, her heart bore the unimaginable weight of sorrow and agony. Yet, she stood firm, embodying a silent strength that spoke volumes more than words could. In that harrowing moment, the prophesy of Simeon—that a sword would pierce her soul—was fulfilled, and through it, she demonstrated the zenith of maternal fortitude. The seamless fabric of her courage and fortitude woven together becomes an enduring shield for all who seek her intercession.

Such virtues are not limited to mythic realms of divine narrative; they are accessible and imperative for all believers. Courage, in the Marian sense, is not merely about heroics in times of overt crisis. It is often quieter, manifesting in the day-to-day decisions to align one's life with God's will. Mary's example shows us that true courage may involve the grace of accepting the unknown and the uncharted, trusting that God's plan, however mysterious, is always wrought with grace.

Practicing fortitude in our contemporary lives means remaining steadfast in the face of trials and adversities. It is the moral muscle that allows us to bear the burdens we encounter, whether they stem from physical suffering, emotional hardships, or spiritual battles. The fortitude of Mary, mirrored in our lives, shapes our perseverance, reminding us that God's strength is our shelter. In this brand of resilience, each act of courage and fortitude becomes an echo of Mary's own life, a small but crucial reflection of her unwavering spirit.

To truly understand the depth of Mary's courage and fortitude, one must recognize the theological underpinnings of her existence. Her Immaculate Conception, which preserved her from original sin, endowed her with a purity and clarity of heart that made her uniquely receptive to God's grace. This grace, in turn, fortified her soul against the fears and sorrows of the world. The courage and fortitude she exhibited are divine gifts, yet they are gifts that can also be cultivated through prayer, sacraments, and a committed relationship with God.

In the philosophical sense, the virtues of courage and fortitude interweave with the concept of ultimate good. Mary's every action and her very life directed toward this ultimate good—union with God. It was this orientation that empowered her to remain courageous and steadfast irrespective of the trials she faced. In our philosophical reflections, we see that true courage and fortitude are not merely human endeavors but are divinely infused qualities directed toward the ultimate purpose of our existence.

As we contemplate these virtues within the context of Marian theology, we are called to internalize and emulate them. Mary's courage calls us to ignite our zeal for living out the Gospel with determination. Her fortitude beckons us to stand firm against the adversities that threaten to shake our faith. In every Mass, every prayer, and every act of charity, we invite Mary's spirit of courage and fortitude to permeate our lives. By doing so, we not only honor her but also increasingly conform our hearts to the Sacred Heart of Jesus, her Son.

In a world rife with uncertainty and suffering, Mary's courage and fortitude shine as beacons of hope and encouragement. For priests, these virtues are particularly crucial. In their pastoral ministry, priests frequently encounter moments that demand the same level of courage and fortitude Mary showed. Whether it is in providing solace to a grieving family, standing up for truth in a world often hostile to it, or guiding the faithful through crisis, Mary's example offers a blueprint for facing these challenges with grace and divine strength.

Moreover, the virtues of courage and fortitude are indispensable in the fight against spiritual apathy and moral relativism. Mary's life exudes a powerful call to spiritual vigilance, urging believers to remain courageous and steadfast in defending and proclaiming the truths of our faith. Her example serves as a powerful antidote to the temptations of discouragement and despair that can so easily ensnare even the most devout souls.

Let us, then, seek Mary's intercession, asking her to illuminate our hearts with the courage and fortitude that she possessed in abundance. As we strive to live out these virtues in our own lives, we fulfill her prophecy that all generations will call her blessed.

By walking in her footsteps, we draw closer to the divine and become vessels of God's grace in a world yearning for hope and strength. Indeed, in exalting Mary's virtues, we not only honor her but also deepen our commitment to the Gospel, transforming our lives into living testimonies of God's boundless love and mercy.

Through meditation on Mary's courage and fortitude, we realize that these virtues are not merely historical or theological concepts but living, breathing realities that can transform our lives. The Blessed Virgin Mary, with her celestial courage and unwavering fortitude, invites us into a deeper communion with God's divine will. In her, we find not just an intercessor, but an exemplar of how to live courageously and steadfastly in our own pursuit of holiness.

As we conclude this reflection, let us carry within us the luminous image of Mary, ever courageous and steadfast. In her radiance, we find the strength to navigate the vicissitudes of our own spiritual journey, secure in the knowledge that her intercession and example will guide us unfailingly toward our ultimate home in the heart of God.

Chapter 7: Scientific Perspectives

In the intricate dance between faith and reason, we find ourselves gazing upon the realm where divine wonders and scientific inquiry intersect. The Blessed Virgin Mary, the epitome of grace and celestial beauty, stands as a beacon of miraculous occurrences that challenge the boundaries of human understanding. From the inexplicable healing powers observed at Marian apparitions to the subtle yet profound connections suggested by the Shroud of Turin, her presence compels both scientists and theologians to pause and marvel. Each miracle attributed to Mary not only fortifies the faith of the devout but also invites the analytical mind to ponder the mysteries beyond empirical evidence. Yet, these scientific perspectives, while striving to unravel the supernatural, often end up affirming the ineffable mysteries of our beloved Mother. Indeed, in the convergence of these worlds, we glimpse the harmony of creation, where empirical scrutiny becomes a bridge leading to the embrace of divine truth.

Miracles Attributed to Mary

The tapestry of Christian faith is woven with threads of wonder and divine intervention, and among these, the miracles attributed to the Blessed Virgin Mary shine with particular luminosity. Her intercessory power is not merely a matter of pious legend but a testament continuously witnessed and confirmed across the ages. In the lilt of prayer and the hush of moments thick with hope, Mary's miraculous presence brings forth life-changing events, proving herself to be the tender Mother of all in their direst needs.

Across centuries, there have been countless reports of physical healings, celestial visions, and inexplicable occurrences attributed to Our Lady's intercession. Think of the miraculous healings at Lourdes, that sanctified ground where Bernadette Soubirous, humble and pure, beheld the beauty of the Immaculate Conception. Pilgrims, struck by maladies that defy medical explanation, find their hopes realized and their bodies restored upon entering those healing waters. The accounts are no mere hearsay; they come documented by neutral medical experts, marking lines where science and the divine touch.

One could imagine Mary standing at the crossroads of heaven and earth, her touch transforming the natural laws that bind our mortal plane. More than just a benefactor of physical cures, Mary appears in the lives of believers through visions radiating celestial wisdom. These visions are not exclusive to saints; ordinary people have found solace in sightings of Our Lady, reporting an indescribable peace and unparalleled direction in their lives thereafter.

Simultaneously tangible and ethereal, Marian apparitions often come with messages resonating divine love and caution—a loving Mother concerned with the wellbeing of her children. The apparitions at Fatima, witnessed by the three shepherd children, brought messages of repentance and prayer. Yet within these somber tones lay a promise of peace and divine providence. The Sun itself danced in the sky, a cosmic ballet reflecting divine approval, witnessed by thousands and leaving even the skeptics stupefied.

Science may ponder and prod, attempting to peel back the layers of these miraculous events. Still, it often stands in reverent silence, unable to fully decipher the heavenly mysteries encapsulated in Mary's workings. In the town of Zeitoun, Egypt, Mary appeared atop a church for weeks, visible to countless onlookers. Radiant and serene, her ethereal figure defied logic and left even non-Christians in awe. What scientific explanation can decode a spectacle that transcends earthly understanding?

The miracles extend beyond the physical realm, touching the very essence of being. In moments of extreme peril, whispered invocations to Mary have brought deliverance and courage. Stories of sailors saved from stormy seas and soldiers protected in battlefields invoke Mary's maternal mantle, as if she sends legions of angels at her command to shield her children from harm. Those who seek her in pleading find their prayers answered in ways unfathomable to clear-eyed rationality.

Moreover, these divine interventions compel believers to reflect on the intricate bond between the natural and supernatural. Here, one sees how Mary, the humble handmaid of the Lord, bridges these realms with her profound, unshakeable love. Her miracles are signposts directing humanity toward God, illuminating the path with celestial light and promises fulfilled through faith.

As advances in modern science push the boundaries of the known universe, they often stumble upon phenomena that elude empirical scrutiny. Here lies a paradox—a silent yet firm nod toward the infinite, manifest in the miracles of Mary. It's as if God allows these occurrences as gentle reminders of His omnipresence, working through His chosen vessel, Mary. They beckon the faithful to recognize the divine operating within the daily confines of human existence, turning the ordinary into a moment of grace.

One such poignant anecdote involves a young woman, bedridden and condemned by medical experts to live out her remaining days in perpetual suffering. Her family, desperate and faithful, turned to Mary with an unwavering hope. Their prayers were answered in a surge of unforeseen strength as the woman stood, restoring not only her body but rejuvenating the faith of an entire community. Such stories ripple through the tapestry of Marian devotion, each stitch a testament to her wondrous intercession.

Mary's miraculous interventions call upon the believer to witness and share the glory of God's love as expressed through His Mother. The skeptic may ask for scientific validation, yet faith requires acknowledgment of mystery, the unseen hand that orchestrates more than meets the eye. Mary, in her divine humility, acts without need for recognition or praise—bearing the reflection of her Son's love and divine mercy.

As we delve deep into the realm of her miracles, one cannot ignore the dual aspect of these divine acts—healing and conversion. She does not merely restore physicalight maladies but also transforms hearts, turning souls toward God in acts of profound conversion. Witness the hardened sinner, reconciled through Marian intercession, setting forth on a path of newfound holiness. It is here that Mary's miracles touch the eternal soul, guiding it toward salvation.

The Church thus rejoices in these manifestations, using them as foundations for greater devotion and deeper spiritual reflection. In her, one sees not only a wonder-worker but a loving Mother, ever inclined to aid, comfort, and lead her children to eternal bliss. Let her miracles, then, be not just marvels of a bygone era but living testimonies, continually urging the faithful toward an intimate union with the divine.

The Shroud of Turin and Marian Connections

In the realm of sacred relics, the Shroud of Turin stands as a mystical artifact, one that inspires awe and contemplation. This linen cloth, which purports to bear the image of Jesus Christ, invites inexorable intrigue, not only for its connection to the divine Passion but also for the subtle threads that link it to the Blessed Virgin Mary. It is in these connections that we find a tapestry woven by grace, inviting us to reflect upon the profound relationship between Mary and the mystery of the Resurrection.

The Shroud's enigmatic existence presents an interplay between faith and science, a dance between the material and the metaphysical. For Roman Catholics, the Shroud is both a witness to the suffering of Christ and a symbol of faith in His Resurrection. But beyond its immediate symbolism, we are drawn to consider its implications for Marian devotion. The tender heart of Mary, who bore Jesus in her womb and stood steadfast at the foot of the Cross, is imbued with a profound connection to the Shroud. She who wrapped her son in swaddling clothes and later witnessed His linen burial cloth carries a poignant, maternal connotation that cannot be overlooked.

From a theological and philosophical perspective, examining the Shroud of Turin invites us to delve into the essence of Mary's role as the New Eve. Just as she is intimately linked to the

Incarnation, she is inherently connected to the Resurrection. The Shroud, bearing the imprint of Christ's passion, evokes Mary's indispensable participation in the salvific process. Here, we are reminded of her Fiat— her unwavering 'yes'—an echo resounding through the ages, culminating in the ultimate sacrifice of her Son.

Speculatively, one may ponder whether the Shroud serves as an esoteric bridge, harmonizing Mary's Immaculate Heart with the Sacred Heart of Jesus. This sacred relic calls us, in hushed whispers, to discern the mysteries of Marian intercession. The cloth reminds us how Mary bore the sorrows of the world, intertwining her sufferings with the redemptive agony of Christ. Our devotion to Mary is deepened through the contemplation of this relic, as it draws us closer to her sorrow and triumph in God's divine plan.

The Shroud's peculiar scientific aspects—such as the unexplained nature of the image's formation, believed to be a result of radiant energy—can be approached through the lens of Marian grace. Can we consider that Mary, chosen and prepared by God, partakes in these miraculous phenomena as a vessel of divine will? As we unravel the Shroud's mysteries, it becomes a catalyst for deepening our reverence for Mary's unique role in salvation history. The convergence of faith and scientific inquiry itself may echo Mary's role as Mediatrix, reconciling heaven and earth through her intercession.

The maternal dimension of the Shroud also invites us to meditate on Mary's assumption into Heaven. The same almighty power that transformed the Shroud's image can be seen as elevating Mary's physical self into heavenly glory. In this light, the Shroud becomes a silent testament not only to Christ's divine victory over death but also to Mary's Assumption, foretasting the resurrection promised to all of God's children. Here, scientific wonder ushers us into a spiritual journey, magnifying our devotion to Mary as the Assumed Queen of Heaven.

To stand before the Shroud is to confront the tangible reality of Christ's passion and resurrection, but it is also to perceive the shadow of a mother's love imprinted invisibly within its folds. Mary's Immaculate Heart, pierced by the sorrows of her Son's suffering, finds an echo in the silent witness of the Shroud. The relic reaches into the depths of Marian devotion, elevating our understanding of her role in the divine mystery.

One must also consider the Shroud as an instrument of Marian evangelization, providing a visual and scientific testimony that complements the spiritual narrative handed down through the ages. The Shroud becomes an icon of both holy suffering and exaltation, converging at the nexus of Christ and Mary. Its mystery transcends borders, inviting skeptics and believers alike to ponder the divine truths it enshrouds.

The synthesis of Marian insights derived from the Shroud's enigmatic presence is not merely an academic exercise but a spiritual pilgrimage. As we venerate this relic, our hearts are lifted to a higher plane of Marian devotion, encouraging us to emulate her virtues—her humility, obedience, and unwavering faith. The Shroud beckons us to a contemplative understanding of Mary, urging us to draw nearer to her Immaculate Heart through the portals of scientific marvel.

Thus, the Shroud of Turin serves not only as a testament to Christ's Passion and Resurrection but also enriches our devotion to Mary. Through the Shroud, we are invited to a deeper spiritual awakening, one that intertwines the mysteries of Christ and Mary in an inseparable dance of divine love and sacrifice. Each examination of the Shroud's mysteries brings us closer to understanding the tender and powerful role of Mary, the Mother of God, and her everlasting impact on the faithful.

Chapter 8: Homilies on Marian Feasts

In the sacred rhythm of the liturgical year, Marian feasts invite the faithful to contemplate the profound mysteries woven into the tapestry of the Blessed Virgin Mary's life. These feasts, each a luminous gem in the Church's crown, shine with the light of divine grace and maternal tenderness. Consider the Annunciation, where Mary's fiat becomes the dawn of our salvation, her humble assent stirring the uncreated into motion. The Assumption follows, a celestial ballet wherein she, unblemished and stainless, is lifted into the heavenly courts, offering us a glimpse of our own eschatological hope. Then there's the Immaculate Conception, a marvel of divine foresight and love, prefiguring her purity and holiness. Our Lady of Sorrows, cloaked in the sacred grief of the Mater Dolorosa, expands our hearts to understand the cost of redemptive love, her sorrows conjoined with the suffering of her Son. Through these homilies, we are invited to mirror her virtues and to let her gaze guide us, immersing our hearts in the sanctifying beauty of her life. The pulpit, thus, becomes an altar where words transmute into acts of devotion, exalting her, our radiant Mother and Queen.

The Annunciation

The Annunciation, a pivotal moment in salvation history, stands as a luminous beacon of faith and obedience, marking the incarnation of the Logos and the pivotal collaboration between Heaven and Earth. The angel Gabriel, dispatched from the celestial realms, descended to the humble abode of Mary of Nazareth. What transpired in that sacred encounter forever altered the course of human history.

Envision the scene: a modest room, serene and unadorned, where an unassuming young maiden goes about her daily tasks. Without warning, the archangel appeared, radiating a divine brilliance that momentarily halted the flow of time. His words, "Hail, full of grace, the Lord is with thee," echoed an ancient promise, reverberating through the corridors of eternity. In those simple yet profound words, Gabriel heralded the dawn of a new covenant and the Godhead's unparalleled favor upon Mary.

The profound simplicity of Mary's response, "Behold the handmaid of the Lord; be it unto me according to thy word," encapsulates the essence of true obedience and humility. Her fiat, punctuated with serene submission, opened the floodgates of divine grace and allowed the Eternal Word to take flesh. This moment is pregnant with theological significance, revealing the nexus of divine initiative and human cooperation. Without

Mary's 'yes', the incarnation would remain a divine mystery unmanifested.

For centuries, theologians, mystics, and devotees have marveled at the confluence of divine grace and human agency exhibited in the Annunciation. Mary's consent wasn't a passive acquiescence but an active embrace of God's plan, woven seamlessly into her immaculate will. Her unique role as the Theotokos – the God-bearer – serves as an unparalleled model of fidelity and divine union.

In Mary's response, we discern the virtue of humility in its purest form. She did not question her worthiness nor seek validation; her soul transcended self-doubt, resting securely in Divine Providence. Mary's humility wasn't merely the absence of pride but a radiant acknowledgment of God's preeminence in all things. This stands as a stark contrast to the pride of the first Eve, highlighting Mary's unique role as the New Eve, ushering redemption through her obedience.

Ponder also on the angelic salutation, "full of grace." These words are not mere ceremonial pleasantries but a revelation of Mary's unique sanctity. From the moment of her Immaculate Conception, Mary was preserved from original sin, making her a vessel pure enough to bear the Holy One. The grace that filled her was not only prevenient but also exhaustive, crowning her as the mediatrix of graces, from whose life the light of divine wisdom and charity stream forth.

The Annunciation invites us to reflect on the intimate union between divine omnipotence and human receptivity. God, in His infinite wisdom, chose to enter into creation not with a show of force but through the gentle acquiescence of a humble virgin. This divine humility, complementing Mary's own, forms the bedrock of salvific history, emphasizing the synergy between Creator and creature.

Moreover, Mary's role in the Annunciation exemplifies the theological principle of co-redemption. By her consent, she participates uniquely in the salvific mission of her Son. Her fiat directly aligns with the divine will, embodying the perfect disciple who hears the Word of God and keeps it. Thus, Mary's role is not merely passive but active, co-operating in God's redemptive plan.

The liturgical celebration of the Annunciation serves as a solemn reminder of this divine mystery, inviting the faithful to a deeper contemplation of Mary's virtues and the incarnational mission of Christ. Each year, the feast on March 25th offers a renewed opportunity to marvel at the astonishing grace, humility, and obedience illuminated in that sacred moment. It rekindles our devotion and draws us closer to the maternal heart of Mary, whose example we strive to imitate.

From a philosophical perspective, the Annunciation raises profound questions about freedom, grace, and human agency. It invites us to ponder the paradox of an omnipotent God seeking consent from His creature. Yet, in Mary's free response, we perceive the harmonization of divine sovereignty and human freedom. This mystery challenges us to fathom the depths of God's condescension and the heights of human cooperation in the economy of salvation.

Additionally, the spiritual implications of the Annunciation are vast. It serves as a perpetual reminder that in moments of uncertainty, God's grace suffuses our lives, enabling us to respond to divine promptings with courage and faith. Mary's example encourages us to cultivate a disposition of receptivity and docility to the Holy Spirit, allowing God's will to manifest through our daily actions and choices.

Thus, the Annunciation is not merely a historical or theological event but a perpetual call to align our wills with God's, to echo Mary's fiat in our lives. It beckons us to recognize and respond to the divine presence that seeks to dwell within us, transforming our hearts into sanctuaries of grace and obedience. The resonance of Gabriel's greeting and Mary's humble assent continues to call forth a deeper commitment to our Christian vocation.

In conclusion, the Annunciation encapsulates the epitome of Marian virtues and the profound theandric mystery of the Incarnation. It transcends mere historical recounting, beckoning us into the depths of divine love and human response. Through the lens of this event, we glimpse the eternal interplay of grace and freedom, inviting us to emulate Mary's unwavering faith and docility. As we meditate on this profound mystery, may our hearts, like Mary's, become fertile ground for God's Word, bearing fruit in perfect harmony with His divine will.

The Assumption

The mystery of The Assumption of the Blessed Virgin Mary is a luminous thread woven through the tapestry of Catholic tradition, one that elevates our understanding of her sanctified role in salvation history. It is a moment where heaven kisses earth, as Mary, the Mother of God, is assumed body and soul into heavenly glory. This dogma, defined by Pope Pius XII in 1950, signifies more than a mere safeguard against the corruption of the tomb; it is a mystical elevation that completes the cycle of her earthly pilgrimage.

The Assumption is not only a commemoration of Mary's journey from earthly life to celestial existence but also an emblem of the divine promise of our own resurrection. Through her Assumption, Mary embodies our ultimate destiny and prefigures our eventual glorification. In her, we witness the fulfillment of God's promise to humanity. "Where she is," as numerous saints have often reflected, "we hope to be one day." This eschatological dimension instills a profound sense of hope and encourages us to aspire to live in sanctity.

Rich in symbolism, the Assumption should be seen not as an isolated event but as an extension of the incredible mysteries that precede it. The Immaculate Conception prepared her for her divine maternity; her perpetual virginity underscored her singular devotion to God. Her Assumption, therefore, is the culmination of a life lived in perfect harmony with the Divine Will. She is the new Ark of the Covenant, who bore not the tablets of the law but the Lawgiver Himself. Her elevation into heaven honors her unique participation in the Incarnation.

Consider the poetic grandeur of this moment: Angels are said to have sung jubilant hymns, their voices blending into celestial symphonies as they escorted Mary to her eternal abode. One might even imagine the stars aligning to form a brilliant pathway, a luminescent road leading her to the throne of the Almighty. Thus, Mary's Assumption enriches our imaginations and draws us into the realm of the sublime, where the natural and the supernatural meet in divine convergence.

Philosophically, the Assumption invites us to ponder the union of body and soul in heavenly bliss. It's a reminder that salvation is not merely spiritual; it encompasses our entire being. Mary's Assumption offers us a glimpse of what awaits the faithful: a restoration and glorification that transcends the merely spiritual, extending to our physical selves as well. In a world often beset by a dichotomy between body and spirit, her Assumption serves to unify these dimensions in holy synchronicity.

The Assumption also exemplifies the profound respect God has for human free will and cooperation in His divine plan. Mary, who humbly accepted the angel's message with a fiat, was taken up into heaven as a testimonial of God's recognition of sanctified human agency. This elevates her role while also reminding us of the importance of our own choices and cooperation with grace.

From a theological perspective, Mary's Assumption is an extension of the divine love and reverence that God holds for His mother. It is an ineffable grace granted to the one who bore Christ, making her the Queen of Heaven and the most exalted of creatures. Her Assumption underscores her role as a powerful intercessor, standing in proximity to her Son, constantly advocating for the souls of the faithful.

The Assumption, then, becomes an invitation for all believers to deepen their devotion to Mary. It beckons us to venerate her not merely as an ancient relic of faith but as a living, glorified presence in our spiritual lives. Through Marian devotions, such as the Rosary and the Angelus, we draw closer to Mary, and through her, to Christ Himself. The Assumption encourages the faithful to see Mary as a model of virtue, inspiring us to live lives that are pure, faithful, and devoted.

While the Church's dogmatic proclamation of the Assumption is relatively recent, the belief has permeated the consciousness of the faithful for centuries. The Assumption has been celebrated in art, literature, and liturgy long before its dogmatic recognition.

Early Church Fathers, mystics, and theologians have all alluded to her heavenly glorification, reflecting the Church's ancient and organic recognition of this divine mystery.

Let us not overlook the mystical aspect of Mary's Assumption, a realm where tangible truths blend with transcendent mysteries. Imagine the awe that the apostles would have felt if they had witnessed her Assumption—a divine seal affirming her immaculate purity and unwavering faith. The serene culmination of her life serves as a mystical reminder of the power and fruits of a life wholly surrendered to God.

In conclusion, The Assumption of the Blessed Virgin Mary is a testament to the divine unity of love, faith, and hope, serving as a luminous beacon for the faithful. Its celebration calls us to reflect deeply on the love of God and the promises He has made to us through Mary. As we contemplate her Assumption, may our hearts be filled with awe and reverence, inspired to pursue holiness with zeal, knowing that our ultimate destiny lies in heavenly communion with our Blessed Mother and her Son.

The Immaculate Conception

The doctrine of the Immaculate Conception is a luminous truth that illuminates the very heart of Marian theology. It captivates the intellect with its profundity and enchants the soul with its beauty. This singular grace granted to the Blessed Virgin Mary by the Almighty Himself reflects the divine wisdom and love that extends beyond the boundaries of human comprehension. Within the context of this sacred feast, celebrated with rejoicing by the Church, we find the essence of purity and divine predestination that is unsurpassed.

It is imperative to understand that the Immaculate Conception does not refer to the miraculous conception of Jesus in Mary's womb, but rather, to Mary's own conception. From the very first moment of her existence, she was preserved exempt from the stain of original sin. This sublime mystery underscores the sanctity and unique role of Mary in God's salvific plan. Her soul, untainted by sin, was made a fitting dwelling place for the Incarnate Word. In this act of divine grace, we observe the prelude to the Incarnation.

The Immaculate Conception was definitively pronounced as dogma by Pope Pius IX in 1854 through the papal bull *Ineffabilis Deus*. The Holy Father declared, "We declare, pronounce, and define that the doctrine which holds that the most Blessed Virgin

Mary, in the first instance of her conception, by a singular grace and privilege granted by Almighty God, in view of the merits of Jesus Christ, the Savior of the human race, was preserved free from all stain of original sin, is a doctrine revealed by God and therefore to be believed firmly and constantly by all the faithful." This proclamation was not an innovation, but rather a crystallization of a belief held in the Church through centuries of tradition and theological reflection.

The Marian feast of the Immaculate Conception, celebrated on December 8, invites the faithful to reflect on the mystery of God's providence and the incomparable holiness of the Mother of God. It is a day that echoes the angelic salutation, "Hail, full of grace, the Lord is with thee" (Luke 1:28). These words of the Archangel Gabriel point towards Mary's pre-sanctification, her being "full of grace" from the very moment of her existence.

In contemplating the Immaculate Conception, we are drawn to the depths of God's mercy and the profound wisdom of His redemptive plan. God, in His omniscience, foresaw the fall of man and ordained the means of salvation. In His infinite love, He chose Mary to be the Ark of the New Covenant, the vessel of divine grace, who would bear the Savior of the world. Her immaculate state was necessary, for the sinless Son of God could only be born of a sinless mother. Through this divine prevenience, the path for the Savior was prepared, allowing the Incarnation to unfold in the fullness of purity and holiness.

Mary's immaculate nature also serves as a model and a beacon of hope for all Christians. In her, we see the possibility of a life wholly dedicated to God, untouched by sin. While we, too, are called to holiness, the challenges of the fallen human condition often besiege us. However, Mary's Immaculate Conception reassures us that God's grace is powerful and transformative. It reminds us that, through His grace, we too can strive towards purity and virtue, always aiming to mirror the divine model presented by our blessed Mother.

Saints and theologians across the ages have spoken eloquently about the Immaculate Conception. St. Thomas Aquinas pondered the fittingness of Mary being sinless, and Duns Scotus ardently defended the doctrine, insisting on the preemptive power of Christ's redemption. These theological reflections culminate in a harmonious symphony that magnifies the glory of the Immaculate Conception, portraying it as a divine necessity and an act of foreseen merit.

Moreover, the apparition of Our Lady of Lourdes to St. Bernadette in 1858 further authenticated the dogma. When the Blessed Virgin identified herself as the Immaculate Conception, the faithful were given a celestial confirmation of the truth proclaimed by the Church. These apparitions fueled the devotional fervor of the faithful and provided a tangible encounter with this sublime mystery.

It is also a profound reminder of the mystery of God's will and how He chooses the humble and the lowly to manifest His glory. Mary's humble and immaculate origin stands in stark contrast to the grandeur we often associate with divine favor. In her lowliness, we see the exaltation of God's wisdom—a wisdom that exalts what the world deems insignificant and crowns it with eternal glory.

In our own spiritual journeys, the Immaculate Conception encourages us to seek God's grace tirelessly. It nurtures our devotion, compelling us to turn often to Mary, asking her to intercede for us so that we may grow in virtue and holiness. She, our sinless mother, standing before God, a testament to His saving power, invites us to trust in God's mercy and to strive towards our heavenly calling with unwavering faith.

Let us, therefore, with hearts aflame, honor this sublime mystery of the Immaculate Conception, rejoicing in the pure and holy Mother given to us. In venerating Mary, we draw closer to Christ, for her life is a reflection of His grace. May our devotion to the Immaculate Conception lead us to a deeper love for God and a renewed commitment to living according to His holy will.

As priests and lay faithful, let us preach and propagate the greatness of this dogma, leading our communities in understanding and reverence. The feast of the Immaculate Conception is not merely an observance but a profound invitation to enter into the mystery of divine love and grace. It is a call to imitation, a clarion whispering to our souls, "Be holy, for I am holy." In our homilies and prayers, may the Immaculate Conception shine forth as a beacon, guiding us towards a life of sanctity and divine communion.

And so, as we meditate on this glorious mystery, may we find ourselves wrapped in the seamless mantle of Mary's purity, seeing in her the reflection of God's perfect love. Let every heart echo the joy of this divine grace, elevating our thoughts to the heavenly realms where the Immaculate Mother reigns in eternal glory..

May our lips never tire of singing her praises, and may our lives forever testify to the transforming power of the Immaculate Conception.

Our Lady of Sorrows

The figure of Our Lady of Sorrows stands as a poignant and heart-wrenching testament to the depth of Mary's fidelity and love for her Divine Son and her suffering alongside the Redeemer. Her sorrows, often encapsulated in the image of her with seven daggers piercing her heart, invoke a profound meditation on the intimate union between Mother and Son in the economy of salvation.

From the proclamation of Simeon, who foretold that a sword would pierce her soul (Luke 2:35), to the harrowing hours spent at the foot of the Cross, Our Lady of Sorrows embodies a living sacrifice, a heart rendered in perfect obedience and unfathomable agony. These seven sorrows, each a station of grief, depict not a distant tragedy but an immediate, living testament to the price of Divine Love.

Her sorrow began in the Temple, where Simeon's prophecy marked the beginning of a long path of suffering. How deep and mysterious is this foresight! A mother, filled with joy at the dedication of her firstborn to the Lord, is suddenly overshadowed by a prophecy that alludes to the ultimate sacrifice. It was a gaze into an abyss that would only grow darker with each passing year.

The flight into Egypt was the second dagger. Mary, holding the tender child Jesus close to her heart, witnessed the world's hostility towards the Incarnate Word. A night filled with haste and fear, driven by obedience to God's command and fueled by the love for Her Son. Every step in the desert sands was accompanied by unspoken cries of a mother braving exile for the safety of the Divine Child.

In the story of the loss of Jesus in the Temple, the third sorrow, Mary's heart beat wildly in panic and worry. The three days of searching, reminiscent of the three days Christ would spend in the tomb, was a foretaste of the separation to come. Her feelings of abandonment and helplessness stand as a universal human experience, transforming this specific sorrow into a shared pilgrimage of every soul seeking the lost Child in the temple of its heart.

The fourth sorrow, meeting Jesus on the way to Calvary, tears at the very fabric of the heart. Seeing her Son, beaten and scourged, carrying the weight of the world's sins in the form of the wooden Cross, Mary's eyes met His. It was a moment that spoke without words, a transcendent exchange of unutterable love and pain. Every tremor of Jesus' burdened steps resonated within her, creating a unified paschal symphony of suffering and redemption.

Standing at the foot of the Cross, the fifth sorrow, Mary witnessed the culmination of agony. The anguish of seeing her beloved Son nailed, drawing His last breaths, forged an eternal bond of compassion between the Immaculate Heart and the Sacred Heart. Every cry of pain, every drop of blood was shared in the ineffable silence of suffering love. Her acceptance of John as her son signified the universal motherhood of all humanity and a new dimension of her sorrow—transformative and redemptive.

The sixth sorrow, the deposition from the Cross, holds within it the overwhelming image of the Pieta. Mary cradling the lifeless body of Jesus, reminiscent of the Nativity, yet now suffused with the profound sorrow of loss. Holding the weight of salvation in her arms, she embraced the fulfillment of God's will in the very death of her Son, as her tears sanctified the wood of the cross and the ground below.

The final sorrow, Jesus' burial, sees her letting go, submitting entirely to the Father's will. This ultimate relinquishment, burying her hope, is the epitome of her unwavering faith. The stone rolled in front of the tomb was not the end but the sacred silence before the dawn of Resurrection. Here, sorrow reaches its zenith, but it is a silence filled with trust in God's promise.

Reflecting on Mary's sorrows invites the believer into a deep communion with the mysteries of Christ's Passion. She did not simply witness these sorrows; she participated in them. This co-suffering turns her into the compassionate mother of all believers, who understand that through her sorrows, a fountain of grace flows. Her motherhood is not a remote, passive title. It's active, engaging, bringing solace to a suffering world through the sheer power of her Immaculate Heart.

The devotion to Our Lady of Sorrows is an invitation to delve into the mystery of redemptive suffering. It illuminates that true discipleship demands an interior crucifixion, a full embrace of God's will, even when it pierces the soul. Such devotion nurtures and intensifies the resolve to take up one's cross, inspired by Mary's silent consent to the divine plan.

In the midst of a world often reluctant to face suffering, Our Lady offers a transformative gaze. Her sorrows suggest that purest joy comes not in the avoidance of pain but in its embrace for the sake of love. This path may seem arduous, but guided by Our Lady's example, it leads to a participation in the Resurrection. Every dagger, each sorrow, serves as a reminder that the substance of love is sacrifice, and through her sufferings, we too encounter Christ.

Consecrating oneself to Our Lady of Sorrows aligns the soul with a reality deeply woven into the tapestry of the human experience—all suffering, touched by grace, becomes a portal into divine mystery. As we contemplate the seven daggers, may our hearts also open to embrace a life patterned after her unyielding faith and love. Let Mary's sorrows transform our sorrows, uniting them with the redeeming Christ, and lead us into the luminous presence of God.

Chapter 9: Hymns in Honor of Mary

As the celestial notes of hymns rise in honor of Mary, they weave a tapestry of divine adulation that transcends time and space. The melodies, borne aloft on the wings of faith, enfold the Blessed Virgin in a luminous aura of reverence and love. Ancient chants such as the "Ave Maria" and contemporary compositions alike pay homage to her unparalleled virtues. These hymns, whether whispered in the quiet sanctity of personal devotion or resounding through the arches of grand cathedrals, become vessels of grace, carrying the heart's deepest yearnings to Heaven's Queen. Through lyrical verses and harmonious cadences, the faithful encounter Mary not just as a distant figure but as a tender mother enveloping them in her maternal embrace. Each note and word, carefully chosen and lovingly offered, becomes a prayer, a plea, and a praise, weaving together the faithful into a communion of souls devoted to the exaltation of the Blessed Virgin Mary.

Traditional Marian Hymns

Throughout the centuries, the faithful have turned to song to express their veneration for Mary, the Mother of God. Traditional Marian hymns occupy a revered place within Catholic liturgical life, embodying a rich tapestry of devotion and theological reflection. They are not merely musical compositions but vehicles of spiritual grace, speaking to the heart in a language that transcends time and space. In these hymns, the glory of Mary is painted in hues of reverence, joy, and sorrow, reflecting the various facets of her divine motherhood and immaculate purity.

One of the most iconic traditional Marian hymns is "Ave Maria," which, in its many versions, invokes the angelic greeting to Mary and petitions her intercession. The melody, whether in the haunting strains of Gregorian chant or the sublime compositions of Schubert and Gounod, elevates the soul to contemplate the mystery of the Incarnation. When Catholics sing "Ave Maria," they join the angel Gabriel in acknowledging Mary's unique role in salvation history and ask for her maternal protection.

Another hymn that resonates deeply within Catholic liturgy is "Salve Regina." Birthing from the heart of monastic piety in the Middle Ages, this hymn tenderly addresses Mary as "Mother of Mercy" and "our life, our sweetness, and our hope." Each verse of

"Salve Regina" is a poetic homage, encapsulating the Church's enduring confidence in Mary's intercession. The hymn's closing appeals—"turn then, most gracious Advocate, thine eyes of mercy toward us"—reflect the faithful's trust in Mary's compassionate guidance and intercession in their earthly pilgrimage.

"Regina Caeli," the joyous anthem of Eastertide, encapsulates the triumph of the Resurrection and Mary's role in it. Sung during the Paschal season, this hymn radiates exultation as it calls on Mary, the Queen of Heaven, to rejoice in her Son's victory over death. The hymn's jubilant melody and verses break forth like a dawning sunrise, illuminating the profound connection between Christ's Resurrection and Mary's exaltation.

Moreover, the ancient hymn "Sub Tuum Praesidium," with its origins tracing back to the early centuries of Christianity, echoes the timeless plea for Mary's protection. The phrase "We fly to thy protection, O Holy Mother of God" has been a refuge for countless generations, expressing the unwavering reliance of the faithful on Mary amid trials and tribulations. This hymn, with its blend of simplicity and depth, serves as a testament to the enduring faith in Mary's maternal care.

The poetic "Litany of Loreto," often chanted or sung, encompasses a collection of invocations and praises to Mary under various titles. Each appellation—"Mirror of Justice," "Seat of Wisdom," "Gate of Heaven"—unveils a facet of Mary's role in the divine economy. The litany's rhythmic cadence weaves a garland of prayers, each petition a blossom of love and devotion offered to the Mother of God. It not only underscores Mary's multifaceted roles but also invites the faithful to ponder her virtues and emulate them.

In times of sorrow, Catholics turn to the deeply evocative "Stabat Mater," a hymn that contemplates Mary's sorrow as she stood by the Cross of her Son. The hymn's poignant verses and somber melody invite the faithful to unite their own sufferings with those of Mary and Jesus. "Stabat Mater" leads the heart through a spiritual journey of empathy, sorrow, and ultimately, hope, reflecting on the redemptive pain borne by the Holy Mother.

Various hymns dedicated to the liturgical feasts of Mary further enrich this tradition. On the feast of the Immaculate Conception, hymns like "Tota Pulchra Es" celebrate Mary's sinless purity, a testament to the divine grace that preserved her from original sin. These hymns not only honor Mary but also illuminate doctrinal truths, educating the faithful through melodious teachings embedded in liturgical celebrations.

"Magnificat," the canticle of Mary, sung traditionally during Vespers, encapsulates Mary's own words of praise to God. This hymn, drawn directly from the Gospel of Luke, offers a glimpse into Mary's soul, imbued with humility and profound gratitude. The "Magnificat" is a hymn of social justice and divine reversal, proclaiming the mighty deeds of God through the lowliness of His handmaid. In singing this canticle, the Church honors Mary's role in salvation and echoes her praise for God's enduring mercy.

The preservation and perpetuation of these hymns are pivotal in maintaining the vibrancy of Marian devotion. Each melody and verse is a conduit through which the faithful encounter Mary's maternal presence and intercession. In communal and personal prayer, these traditional Marian hymns resound as an enduring testament to the love and reverence bestowed upon the Blessed Virgin.

The beauty and theological depth of traditional Marian hymns cannot be overstated. They encapsulate the mystery of Mary's life, her divine motherhood, and her intimate participation in the redemptive mission of Christ. These hymns serve to bridge the temporal with the eternal, lifting hearts and minds to ponder the ineffable grace bestowed upon Mary and, through her, to all humanity.

As such, traditional Marian hymns remain an essential element of Catholic prayer and worship, fostering a profound and affective devotion to Mary. They are not mere relics of the past but living expressions of faith, continually inviting the Church to contemplate the mystery and majesty of the Mother of God. Each note, each word, is an invocation of Mary's ceaseless intercession and a testament to her enduring presence in the life of the Church.

Original Compositions

The vast and boundless waters of Marian devotion carry within their depths the echoes of countless hymns, both ancient and new. Among these, the section set apart for Original Compositions emerges like fresh springs, bubbling up from the soul's profound wellspring. Within these compositions, the poets and hymnists of our age dare to touch upon the ineffable beauty of the Blessed Virgin, to express in their own humble ways the love and veneration she inspires.

Each new hymn, lovingly crafted, seeks to give voice to the ineffable mysteries of Mary's holy life. Just as a painter spills his emotions onto a canvas, so too does the hymnist pour their reverence into each note and lyric. These Original Compositions are not merely artistic endeavors; they are acts of worship, imbued with heartfelt supplication, praise, and the longing of the soul to dwell closer to Mary. They strive to capture the transcendent, to bridge the celestial with the terrestrial through the sublime medium of music and poetry.

Consider the tender quatrains that whisper of the Annunciation, where the angel's greeting is transformed into melody, trembling with the awe of Gabriel's message. Or the solemn hymns of the Crucifixion, wherein the sorrows of Mary standing at the foot of the Cross echo through chords that resonate with the very lament of Heaven. These compositions are the sacred vessels bearing the story of Mary's joy and grief, her divine motherhood, and her role as the spiritual mother of all humanity.

Poetic in their essence, these hymns often employ the language of allegory and metaphor. Mary's virtues are likened to an immaculate rose, a beacon of unwavering light, a sanctuary of divine wisdom. Through the alchemy of words and music, Mary becomes not only a figure from sacred history but the living, breathing queen of our hearts, ever-present and ever-inviting us to profound intimacy with the divine.

In these Original Compositions, the creative spirit of the composers mirrors the divine creativity of Mary's own fiat. Their work stands as a testament to the inexhaustible source of inspiration that Mary provides to the faithful. Each new hymn is a fresh Ave Maria, a modern Magnificat, breathing new life into age-old devotions. Modern technology, too, plays its part; with digital means and the internet, these compositions find their way across the globe, resonating in sacred spaces they might never have reached before.

The spiritual architects of these hymns often draw upon Marian apparitions and miraculous events as their muse. One can hear the echo of Lourdes' gentle spring, the serenity of Fatima's fields, the solemnity of Guadalupe's tilma, encapsulated in the notes of these compositions. These hymns become a convergence point where historical Marian events and today's devout expressions forge an unbreakable chain of continuity and devotion.

Rewriting the magnificence of Mary in new hymns embodies a pilgrimage of the soul, a journey that both hymn-writer and listener undertake together. These contemporary acts of devotion whisper gently into the ears of a distracted world, calling it back to contemplation and reverence of Mary. They serve as a harmonious bridge connecting the doctrinal, the mystical, and the experiential aspects of Marian devotion.

As the faithful recite these hymns, the vibrations of their collective voices rise like incense, ascending into heavens already fragrant with the prayers of saints. Through the lens of poetic imagination, the everyday struggles and triumphs of Mary become relatable moments, lived and relived in the sanctuaries of our hearts. These songs often explore Mary's journey from a human perspective—her doubts, her fears, and her ultimate surrender to divine will.

Sometimes these compositions grapple with Mary's silence, her contemplative nature, pondering each word in her heart. They invite the congregation to step into this sacred silence, to find solace in the unspoken, to experience the divine mystery that words alone cannot capture. Through such reflective compositions, we access that quiet room where Mary receives the angel's salutation, where she ponders the shepherds' adoration, and where her immaculate heart is entwined with her son's suffering.

The devotion embedded in these Original Compositions also finds expression in varied musical styles, merging the traditional with the contemporary. Gregorian chants might intertwine with modern orchestration, creating a timeless tapestry of sound. Liturgical choirs might blend into acoustic ballads, making Marian hymns accessible to diverse congregational tastes. This musical adaptability ensures Mary's praise resounds through varied cultural and ecclesial landscapes, uniting hearts in singular devotion despite multiplicity.

Such compositions might focus on daily prayers, providing melodies that guide the faithful from dawn's first light to the serenity of twilight. They serve as musical anchors anchoring the soul throughout the day, infusing each mundane activity with a sense of the sacred. Morning hymns could echo the initial "Fiat" of Mary, while evening compositions might resonate with her Magnificat, encapsulating daily sacrifices and graces.

Moreover, these hymns celebrate not just universal aspects of Mary but also invite the faithful to ponder her unique role in individual lives. Personal and communal experiences with

Marian intercession find their voice in these hymns, turning testimony into worship. By singing these compositions, the faithful transform personal stories into a universal ode of grace, allowing the majesty of Mary's maternal care to be felt intimately.

The composers of these hymns stand as contemporary heralds, their voices mirroring the angelic choirs that once sang at the dawn of salvation history. In their works, the Holy Spirit breathes anew, inspiring compositions that reflect not just intellectual assent to Marian doctrine but a deep, transformative love. Each note is a petal in the eternal wreath of devotion laid at Mary's feet, a perpetual festival of worship.

The Original Compositions thus become more than songs; they metamorphose into spiritual pathways leading us deeper into the heart of Mary, and through her, to the Sacred Heart of her Son. They whisper of a love that stands vigilant, a motherly embrace that never wanes, urging us onward in our spiritual sojourn with hope, faith, and love. And in this sacred echo, the souls find their eternal home, beautifully suspended in the divine harmony of hymns offered in honor of Mary.

Chapter 10: Marian Prayers and Devotions

In the rich tapestry of Catholic devotion, Marian prayers and devotions stand as vibrant threads, weaving through the spiritual lives of the faithful with a celestial grace. These acts of piety, imbued with a sense of the miraculous and the sublime, elevate the soul toward the divine mysteries of the Blessed Virgin Mary. The rhythmic recitation of the Rosary contemplates the joyous, sorrowful, and glorious mysteries of Christ's and Mary's lives, while the solemn sound of the Angelus brings to mind the incarnate mystery thrice daily, resonating through the hours with angelic whispers. Litanies and novenas rise like incense, invoking Mary's intercession with heartfelt supplication and trust. Each prayer and devotion becomes a poetic dialogue between the soul and the Mother of God, a philosophical act of meditative love that transcends the mundane and opens the heart to eternal truths. Here, in this sacred communion, we find not just solace, but a profound connection to the divine grace that Mary so abundantly dispenses as our Mediatrix and loving Mother.

The Rosary

Amidst the sacred tapestry of Marian prayers and devotions, the Rosary occupies a privileged throne as both a spiritual weapon and a garland woven from the purest intentions of the faithful. Its beads, strung together like a constellation of grace, guide souls through the mysteries of our salvation, each 'Hail Mary' a luminous echo reverberating through the annals of time. The Rosary, in its simplicity and profundity, mirrors the very essence of the Virgin Mary—an arc of humility and grandeur, a silent symphony of faith and contemplation.

It is said that the Rosary was given to Saint Dominic by the Blessed Virgin herself as an antidote to heresy and a beacon of hope in times of darkness. Whether this be embroidered in legend or truth matters little; what remains incontrovertible is its power and efficacy. Every bead we touch, every prayer we mutter, is a step along the pathway to divine union, a tangible thread connecting us to Heaven. The Rosary, though rooted in the soil of human necessity, blossoms into a celestial flower in the garden of the cosmos.

To speak of the Rosary without mentioning its structure would be to paint a halo without light. Consisting of five sets of ten Hail Marys, each decade is introduced by an Our Father and concluded with a doxology. Yet beneath these rhythmic recitations lies a meditative journey through the Joyful, Sorrowful, Glorious, and Luminous Mysteries. Each mystery, a rose offered to Mary, unfolds a scene from the life of Christ and His Blessed Mother, drawing the faithful into a deeper contemplation of divine truths.

The Rosary transforms the soul, reshaping it in the image of Mary's virtues. As one meditates on the Annunciation, the Visitation, the Nativity, and all the luminous events of our faith, the soul imbibes purity, humility, obedience, and a profound sense of divine mission. It awakens a profound empathy for the sufferings of Christ, especially through the Sorrowful Mysteries, where the weight of the Cross grinds us into the grain of compassion and penitence.

In a world often marred by distraction and disconnection, the Rosary serves as a chain of unity, binding the Church Militant to the Church Triumphant. It is the spiritual rosary vine that climbs the trellis of our daily lives, anchoring us to the foundations of faith while reaching ever upward toward the heavens. Such is its mystic allure and timeless relevance.

Each bead is a testament to centuries of devotion, a whisper of countless voices that have turned to Mary in moments of joy and despair. To hold the Rosary is to hold a legacy of faith enshrined in tactile prayer. As fingers move from one bead to another, they traverse the geography of divine love, with the Virgin's hands guiding them steadily.

The Rosary is not merely a repetition of prayers; it is a profound and unceasing dialogue with the Holy Mother. Through the recitation of Hail Mary after Hail Mary, we immerse ourselves in a spiritual rhythm that aligns our hearts with the Immaculate Heart of Mary. This repetitive prayer is akin to a child clinging to the gentle hands of his mother, finding solace and strength in each embrace.

The efficacy of the Rosary lies not only in its words but also in its ability to draw us closer to Mary, who in turn leads us to Her Son. Each mystery is a portal to divine contemplation, grounding us in the temporal reality while transporting our spirits to celestial realms. This is the magic and realism interwoven through its fabric—a mystical ladder that reaches from our daily toil to the heavenly abode.

Philosophically, the Rosary encapsulates the ultimate truths of existence, tracing the arc of salvation history. It begins with the joyful assent to God's will and culminates in the glorious fulfillment of divine promise. In meditating upon these mysteries, we are invited to see the fingerprints of God in our lives, to uncover a layer of sanctity and purpose hidden beneath the mundane.

The temporal recitation of the rosary chains us to eternity. Each prayer breathes life into our spiritual journey, making us vessels of Mary's grace and partakers in her mission. Through the Rosary, Mary becomes not only the Mother of God but our mother, confidante, and intercessor, bringing our petitions before the throne of divine mercy.

The Rosary's poetic cadence transforms our spirit into an instrument of divine praise. Its melodic litanies transcend words to become offerings lifted upon angelic wings. Each "Hail Mary, full of grace" is a brushstroke of love inscribed upon the canvas of our soul, rendering it ever more beautiful in the eyes of God.

In reciting the Rosary, one participates in an ancient tradition of Marian devotion that stretches across ages and cultures. It's this unity of voices in prayer that fortifies the Church, creating a mystical communion of saints and believers. The Rosary is the spiritual heartbeat of Marian devotion, syncing our hearts with the Sacred and Immaculate Hearts.

As one engages with the Rosary, there is an invitation to enter a sanctified space where Heaven touches Earth. Here, Mary's maternal presence enfolds us, and the mysteries of Her life and that of Her Divine Son become a prism through which God's light shines more vividly upon our lives. Through each decade, we are sanctified by Mary's love and Christ's truth.

The Rosary calls us to continual conversion, inspiring a deeper commitment to live out our baptismal vows with renewed fervor. It is an instrument of peace and contemplation, a touchstone that reorients our hearts toward the Divine Will. In these beads and prayers lie an ocean of grace, awaiting the soul that dares to plunge into its depths.

More than a prayer, the Rosary is a living dialogue, a conversation that spans from Earth to Heaven, fusing the temporal with the eternal. In every whispered prayer and every heartfelt meditation, we ascend a spiritual Mount Carmel, where the fire of divine love consumes us, purifies us, and makes us more like Mary, our Mother and Guide.

The Angelus

The Angelus captures a moment of divine interaction, bridging
the eternal with the temporal. This prayer, rich in history and
solemnity, has become a daily ritual for many Roman Catholics,
marking the rhythm of the day with a sacred melody of devotion.
As the church bells toll at morning, noon, and evening, they
invite the faithful to pause and remember the incarnation, that
profound mystery of God-made-man through Mary. The very
essence of The Angelus is deeply rooted in the humility and
obedience of the Blessed Virgin Mary, whose 'Fiat' made the
salvation of humanity possible.

The origins of The Angelus trace back to the monastic tradition
of the Middle Ages. The monks, who centered their lives around
prayer, introduced this devotion as a way to sanctify the different
parts of the day. Initially, it began as a way to recite three Hail
Marys at the evening bell, eventually evolving into the form we
recognize today. The Angelus prayer is a meditative reflection on
the Annunciation, the moment when the Archangel Gabriel
brought the astonishing news to Mary that she would conceive
and bear the Son of God.

*"The angel of the Lord declared unto Mary, and she conceived by the
Holy Spirit."* These words open The Angelus, setting a tone of
reverence and awe. Each phrase of the prayer is infused with a

deep theological significance, guiding the faithful to reflect on the mysteries of the Incarnation. The response, *"Behold the handmaid of the Lord; be it done unto me according to Thy word,"* encapsulates Mary's submission and her exemplary obedience to God's will. This moment of Mary's fiat - a Latin word meaning "let it be done" - resonates deeply within the hearts of the faithful, reminding them of the beauty of surrendering to divine providence.

Following the initial verses, a Hail Mary is recited, amplifying the bond between the faithful and the Holy Mother. The repetition of the Hail Marys serves not as a monotonous chant but as a harmonic echo of devotion, elevating the soul to heavenly contemplation. The richness of the Hail Mary, with its blend of Angelic greeting and Elizabethan prophecy, makes it a profound meditative recitation that not only honors Mary but also acknowledges her pivotal role in salvation history.

The next verse, *"And the Word was made flesh, and dwelt among us,"* ushers in the climax of the Angelus. This declaration of the Incarnation - God taking human form - invites believers to ponder the mystery of the Divine condescension, embracing humanity's frailty yet remaining wholly divine. The accompanying Hail Mary deepens the reflection, anchoring the awe-inspiring reality of the Incarnation in personal devotion. The simple yet powerful imagery of God dwelling among us transforms the mundane into the sacramental, rendering every life event a participation in the divine mystery.

The concluding prayer, *"Pray for us, O Holy Mother of God, that we may be made worthy of the promises of Christ,"* brings the Angelus to a serene and hopeful culmination. This plea for Mary's intercession reflects the longstanding belief in her powerful role as an intercessor. The faith of the Church has long held that as the Mother of God, Mary's prayers are potent and efficacious, bringing grace and help to those who invoke her name with sincere hearts. By relying on Mary's intercession, the faithful seek to align themselves more closely with Christ's promises, nurturing a life of grace and virtue.

The beauty of The Angelus lies not merely in its words but in the rhythm it imparts to daily life. Reciting this prayer at specific times of the day serves as a spiritual anchor, weaving moments of sanctity into the fabric of everyday existence. Whether beginning the day, pausing amid the noon bustle, or reflecting at sunset, The Angelus calls the faithful to a continual remembrance of God's love made manifest through Mary. This rhythmic dedication transforms the cadence of life into a perpetual hymn of praise and gratitude.

Moreover, The Angelus has a profound communal aspect. Traditionally, it was not just an individual's prayer but a collective act of devotion, often recited in families, workplaces, and communities. The angelus bells ringing out in churches served as a call to prayer for everyone within earshot, uniting the community in a shared expression of faith. This communal dimension of The Angelus underscores the universality of Mary's fiat, inviting all believers to join in her assent to God's will.

As we delve deeper into The Angelus, it becomes evident that this prayer is much more than a series of recitations. It is a gateway to a deeper Marian devotion, fostering a profound relationship with the Blessed Virgin. Through The Angelus, believers are drawn into Mary's inner world, her joys, her sorrows, and her unwavering faith. The repetition of the prayer engrains the mysteries of Christ's Incarnation in the hearts of the faithful, making them more receptive to the workings of divine grace.

For priests, The Angelus holds particular significance. This prayer underscores the centrality of Mary in the Church's life and ministry. As shepherds of the faithful, priests have the unique privilege and responsibility to foster Marian devotion within their communities. Reciting The Angelus daily, leading the congregation in this prayer, and elucidating its spiritual depth in homilies and catechesis, priests can nurture a robust Marian spirituality that inspires and strengthens the faith of their flock.

In the cacophony of modern life, The Angelus serves as a timeless reminder of the sacred amid the secular. It calls the faithful to pause and remember the love of a God who chose to become one with humanity through Mary. This brief, yet profoundly rich prayer, offers a moment of stillness and reflection, a moment to reconnect with the divine narrative that shapes our existence. Whether whispered in solitude or sung in the midst of a bustling city, The Angelus transforms time itself into an offering of praise.

The Angelus, in essence, is a symphony of faith. Its simple words resonate with deep theological and spiritual insights, drawing the faithful into a closer relationship with Our Lady and through her to Christ. It is a testimony to the enduring relevance of Marian prayer in the life of the Church, a prayer that, while simple in form, is boundless in its capacity to elevate the soul.

In embracing The Angelus, we embrace Mary's yes - her unreserved submission to God's will, her role in the divine plan of salvation, and her perpetual intercession. In each recitation, we are invited to renew our own fiat, to offer our lives anew to the divine will, and to walk in the humble footsteps of the one who bore the Word made flesh. May The Angelus be more than a prayer; may it be a way of life, a testament of our devotion to Mary, and through her, to our Savior.

Litanies and Novenas

Among the treasures of Marian devotion, litanies and novenas shine like celestial constellations in the spiritual firmament, inviting the faithful to immerse themselves in the profound mysteries and virtues of the Blessed Virgin Mary. These devotions are more than mere recitations; they are intimate dialogues with the Queen of Heaven, punctuated with heartfelt supplications and adorned with lyrical praises.

A litany, derived from the Greek word "litaneia" meaning supplication, is a form of prayer that echoes with the rhythmic cadence of invocation and response. The Litany of Loreto, one of the most venerated litanies in the Roman Catholic tradition, consists of a series of invocations to Mary under her various titles. Each invocation, whether calling upon her as "Holy Mother of God" or "Mirror of Justice", is not merely a title but a testament to her divine motherhood and her role as an exemplar of virtue.

As we recite the Litany of Loreto, we participate in a centuries-old tradition that began in the medieval period at the sanctuary of Our Lady of Loreto in Italy. The litany became popular during the 16th century and was officially approved by Pope Sixtus V. Its poetic beauty lies in the invocation of Mary's many graces, each title unravelling a different facet of her immaculate existence and inviting us to meditate upon her virtues.

Novenas, on the other hand, are nine-day periods of prayer that call upon the faithful to intercede through Mary in various needs and intentions. Rooted in the Latin word "novem" meaning nine, novenas emulate the nine days of prayer that the Apostles and the Virgin Mary herself undertook between the Ascension of Jesus and the descent of the Holy Spirit at Pentecost. Each novena is a pilgrimage of the heart, a journey of faith that brings us closer to the tender intercession of our Heavenly Mother.

Novenas to the Blessed Virgin are as varied as the flowers in a Marian garden, each with its own unique spiritual fragrance. The Novena to Our Lady of Perpetual Help, for instance, seeks Mary's assistance in times of distress and invokes her powerful intercession to obtain temporal and spiritual favors. This particular devotion is deeply cherished by those who find solace in her perpetual and unwavering support.

Another beloved novena is the Novena to Our Lady of the Miraculous Medal, which traces its origins to the apparition of the Virgin Mary to Saint Catherine Labouré in 1830. The devotion promises great graces to those who approach Mary with confidence and wear the medal inscribed with the plea, "O Mary, conceived without sin, pray for us who have recourse to thee."

This novena encapsulates the essence of Marian intercession, highlighting the miraculous power that flows through her maternal care.

One cannot discuss litanies and novenas without embracing their deep philosophical underpinnings. In engaging with these devotions, the faithful enter into a mystical dialogue that transcends the limitations of human language and touches the ineffable. Each prayer, each invocation, is a testament to the intimate relationship between Mary and her children, echoing the love that surpasses all understanding.

In the philosophical realm, litanies and novenas reflect an ontological participation in the divine mystery. They constitute acts of faith that bridge the finite and the infinite, the human and the divine. Through these devotions, the soul is drawn into a deeper communion with the Holy Trinity, as Mary herself is the Theotokos, the God-bearer who leads us to her Son, Jesus Christ.

The theological impact of these devotions is equally profound. Litanies and novenas serve as conduits of divine grace, channeling the inexhaustible mercy of God through the hands of Mary. As the Mediatrix of all graces, her intercession is a powerful testament to her unique role in the economy of salvation. The faithful who invoke her through litanies and novenas experience a tangible connection to the mysteries of salvation and the inexorable love of the Sacred Heart of Jesus.

Furthermore, litanies and novenas possess a transformative power that extends beyond the individual to the ecclesial community. They foster a collective spirit of prayer and unity, drawing the faithful together in a shared expression of devotion. The recitation of the litany before the Blessed Sacrament, or the communal gathering for a novena, solidifies the spiritual bonds within the Body of Christ, reinforcing the unity of the Church under the maternal mantle of Mary.

In reflecting upon these devotions, one cannot overlook their poetic and artistic significance. The rhythmic ebb and flow of litanies, the structured repetition in novenas, and the evocative imagery used in the invocations all contribute to a rich tapestry of Marian artistry. Each word is a brushstroke in the grand painting of Marian devotion, each prayer a verse in the eternal hymn of praise.

Indeed, the traditions of litanies and novenas are complemented by the personal reflections and experiences of countless saints and mystics. Saints such as Alphonsus Liguori, Louis de Montfort, and Mother Teresa have illuminated the path of Marian devotion through their writings and personal testimonies, inspiring the faithful to engage more deeply with these sacred practices.

Ultimately, the practice of litanies and novenas is a testament to the enduring love between Mary and her children. It is a sacred dialogue, a continuous act of faith, and a profound expression of trust in her intercession. It is through these devotions that the faithful are invited to drink from the fountain of grace, to partake in the celestial banquet where Mary presides as the Queen of Heaven.

In conclusion, the litanies and novenas dedicated to the Blessed Virgin Mary offer the faithful a pathway to spiritual enrichment and divine intimacy. They are not merely prayers, but profound invitations to delve deeper into the mysteries of faith, to embrace the virtues of Mary, and to seek her powerful intercession in our lives. Through these devotions, the faithful unite their hearts with the Immaculate Heart of Mary, opening themselves to the boundless graces bestowed by her Son, our Lord Jesus Christ.

Chapter 11: Defending Marian Dogmas

In the luminous tapestry of Marian dogmas, each thread weaves a testament of divine grace and ineffable mystery, echoing through the corridors of time. Poised at the intersection of heaven and earth, these doctrines illuminate the Immaculate Conception, Perpetual Virginity, Assumption, and the divine motherhood of Mary as Theotokos, refining our souls with their celestial brilliance. Embracing both philosophy and theology, these dogmas rise as celestial pinions, bearing testimony to Mary's unparalleled role in God's salvific plan. Recall the wisdom of Sacred Scripture and the diligent teachings of the Early Church Fathers, who, like vigilant sentinels, guard the sanctity of these truths against ephemeral doubts and modern critiques. As the stars punctuate the vast night sky, so do these Marian truths speckle the dark expanse of our doubts, leading us toward unwavering faith. Let us, with the fervor of angels and the docility of children, defend these divine mysteries that God, in His infinite wisdom, has bestowed upon His most favored handmaid.

Common Objections

In the radiant expanse of Marian doctrine, a somber cloud often drifts in, carrying with it the thunders of skepticism and misunderstanding. When we immerse ourselves in the profound mysteries of Marian dogmas, we inevitably encounter a spectrum of objections. Some emerge from theological misapprehensions, others from deeply rooted traditions that diverge from the Catholic faith. Nonetheless, understanding these objections allows us to respond with clarity and compassion, illuminating the truths that lie at the heart of our devotion.

One of the most frequently voiced objections concerns Mary's Immaculate Conception. How, skeptics ask, could Mary have been conceived without original sin when the Scriptures teach that all have sinned and fall short of the glory of God? It is here that we must gently guide these questioners through the theological insight that the Immaculate Conception is not a contradiction of Scripture, but a sublime fulfillment of it. Just as the angel Gabriel proclaimed Mary "full of grace" (Luke 1:28), we understand that this state of being was necessary for her role as the Mother of God. Grace filled her from the start, preserving her from the stain of original sin, preparing her to bear the Divine Word.

Another common objection targets the perpetual virginity of Mary. Critics argue that the New Testament references to Jesus' "brothers" and "sisters" (Mark 6:3) imply that Mary had other children. Yet, the term "brother" in the Hebrew and Aramaic context often referred to close relatives, such as cousins. Analyzing the linguistics and cultural significance of these terms offers a robust defense. Moreover, the Church Fathers, with their intimate connection to apostolic teaching, have unanimously affirmed Mary's lifelong virginity, viewing her as a perpetual temple of the Holy Spirit.

The Assumption of Mary into heaven is another doctrine that evokes skepticism, especially in Protestant circles that emphasize sola scriptura, or "Scripture alone." Detractors claim there is no explicit biblical basis for this belief. However, we must consider the rich tapestry of Sacred Tradition along with Sacred Scripture. The Dormition and Assumption of Mary are not merely pious legends but are rooted in the apostolic witness and the liturgical and devotional life of the early Church. The Assumption is a powerful symbol of the eschatological promise: a preview of the resurrection and glorification that awaits all who are united with Christ.

When considering Mary as Theotokos, or "God-bearer," objections arise primarily from a misunderstanding of Christological truths. Some argue that this title elevates Mary to a quasi-divine status, confusing her with God. To dispel this confusion, we must clarify that calling Mary Theotokos safeguards the doctrine of the Incarnation—that Jesus Christ is fully God and fully man. This title, affirmed at the Council of Ephesus in 431, asserts the unity of Christ's divine and human natures. Mary's role as Theotokos underscores her unique and indispensable participation in the divine plan of salvation.

Another stumbling block is the notion of Mary as Mediatrix of All Graces. Critics contend that it diminishes the unique mediatorial role of Jesus Christ. However, Mary as Mediatrix does not imply she acts independently of Christ; rather, she cooperates with and participates in His singular mediation. Just as the moon reflects the sun's light, Mary reflects the graces of Christ, distributing them as a mother would distribute the resources of the household. Through her, we see an extraordinary channel of divine grace that flows not through her merit but through her willing participation in God's salvific will.

Some find the title of Mary as Co-Redemptrix problematic, interpreting it to mean that Mary is on par with Christ in the redemptive process. However, this interpretation is a gross misunderstanding of the term. To call Mary Co-Redemptrix is to recognize her unparalleled cooperation in the work of redemption. At the foot of the cross, Mary's suffering united with that of her Son, offering her maternal heart in solidarity with His sacrificial love. She is co-redemptive not as an equal partner but as the most intimate participant in Christ's redemptive mission.

The title of Auxiliatrix, or Helper, is sometimes viewed by skeptics as a vestige of earlier, non-Christian goddess worship. Yet, this view fails to acknowledge that Mary's help is firmly rooted in her role as mother and intercessor. The Church's maternal love is embodied in Mary, and her assistance is a testament to her enduring care for humanity. Throughout history, Marian apparitions and intercessions during times of crisis have solidified her role as our spiritual helper, pointing always to her Son and the salvation He offers.

In addressing these objections, it's essential to recognize that the resistance often stems from deep-seated theological positions and historical contexts. Engaging with these arguments requires not only theological acumen but also pastoral sensitivity. We must listen carefully to the concerns of our brothers and sisters, responding not with condemnation but with the gently persuasive light of the Gospel.

The defense of Marian dogmas is not merely an intellectual exercise; it's an invitation to deeper communion with the mysteries of our faith. In lifting our hearts to understand these profound truths, we also elevate our spirits to a higher plane of devotion and love. For every argument raised against the veneration of the Blessed Virgin Mary, a wellspring of grace and understanding flows forth from the Church's rich treasury of wisdom. By addressing these objections thoughtfully and compassionately, we lead others into the radiant embrace of Mary, our Mother, who points always to Christ, our Savior.

Scriptural and Historical Evidence

The Marian dogmas, profound and exalted, are not mere ecclesiastical constructs but are deeply rooted in Scripture and bolstered by the annals of history. The fusion of sacred text with historic testimony creates a rich tapestry, showcasing the divine role of the Blessed Virgin Mary within God's salvific plan.

Holy Scripture provides the cornerstone for our understanding of Mary's unique position. In the Old Testament, the Book of Genesis intimates her significance when God declares enmity between the serpent and the woman. This protoevangelium, the divine foreshadowing, speaks volumes in a mere whisper. Mary emerges as the new Eve, unblemished and obedient, juxtaposed against the fall of the first woman. From this paradigmatic prophecy, the line of scriptural breadcrumbs leads us to the fullness of her grace.

In the New Testament, the angelic salutation illustrates Mary's singular sanctity. "Hail, full of grace" (Luke 1:28) - these words, brimming with celestial significance, denote a state of grace unparalleled. This greeting is not a fleeting moment but a profound testament to Mary's Immaculate Conception. The purity of her being is recognized by an angelic pronouncement, a divine validation that resounds through the ages.

Moreover, consider the Visitation; Elizabeth, filled with the Holy Spirit, proclaims, "Blessed are you among women, and blessed is the fruit of your womb!" (Luke 1:42). These declarations reflect a heavenly orchestration, emphasizing Mary's blessedness in the divine narrative. It is essential to recognize that being "blessed among women" elevates Mary to a unique, singular status among all humankind, underlining her preeminent role from a scriptural vantage point.

Historical evidence complements and enhances scriptural affirmations. The early Church Fathers, steeped in prayer and study, elucidated these scriptural truths. In their writings, we find a consistent affirmation of Marian doctrines. For instance, Saint Irenaeus, in his treatises, firmly identifies Mary as the new Eve, drawing a direct lineage of thought from apostolic teachings to ecclesiastical doctrine.

The tapestry of Christian tradition is interwoven with numerous councils and synods that have deliberated upon and defended Marian dogmas. The Council of Ephesus in A.D. 431 is a pivotal moment. In declaring Mary as Theotokos, the God-bearer, the council reinforced the unity of Christ's divine and human natures while affirming Mary's essential role in salvation history. Such declarations were not mere theological postulates but responses to heretical challenges, fortified by the collective wisdom and spiritual discernment of the Church.

Additionally, the Perpetual Virginity of Mary finds resonance not just in theological assertions but also in historical documentation. Early Christian writers like Saint Jerome rigorously defended this doctrine against detractors, detailing how Mary's virginity is multifaceted, encompassing before, during, and after the birth of Christ. The historical breadth of this belief underscores its deep-rooted acceptance and veneration among the early faithful.

As the centuries unfurled, various Marian apparitions further cemented the historical underpinnings of these dogmas. From Lourdes to Fatima, the Blessed Virgin has revealed herself, her messages consistently calling for prayer, repentance, and devotion. These appearances, witnessed and documented by hundreds, sometimes thousands, underscore her ongoing maternal solicitude for humanity.

Moreover, the Assumption of Mary, though formally declared dogma in 1950 by Pope Pius XII, echoes through centuries of tradition and belief. The historical witness of this dogma can be traced back to the early Church, with writings and homilies that speak of Mary's heavenly assumption. The Dormition traditions in the Eastern Church and the Western devotion to the Assumpta mirror one another, notwithstanding geographic and cultural divides, revealing a universal acknowledgment of this divine truth.

The Coronation of Mary as Queen of Heaven further finds both scriptural and ecclesiastical support. The twelfth chapter of Revelation speaks of a woman clothed with the sun, with the moon under her feet and a crown of twelve stars upon her head. While interpretations vary, the Marian perspective sees this vison as a celestial affirmation of her queenship. Historically, this queenly role has been echoed and celebrated in liturgy, art, and devotion, cementing her sovereign status in the celestial court.

In examining the scriptural and historical evidence, one encounters a harmonious symphony of divine revelation and human affirmation. The scriptural bedrock is indispensable, but the historical witness provides a strong buttress, affirming and elucidating the Church's Marian dogmas. From the echoes of angelic pronouncements to conciliar proclamations, from the vigilant writings of Church Fathers to the miraculous apparitions, the veneration of the Blessed Virgin Mary is neither a fabrication nor a mere tradition.

Rather, it is a profound recognition of her unique role in God's salvific plan, a role that is illuminated by both the light of Scripture and the guidance of history. It is in these twin beacons that the faithful find both assurance and inspiration, venerating Mary not just as the mother of our Lord, but as the Immaculate Conception, the perpetual Virgin, the Assumed and crowned Queen, who intercedes for humanity with a mother's love and a queen's grace. Through Scripture and history, we are invited into the grand narrative of redemption, where Mary's role is not only honored but indispensable.

Chapter 12: Conversion and Commitment

In the ineffable journey towards Marian devotion, the light of personal conversion flickers into a steadfast flame of commitment. This transformation, a divine interplay of grace and will, unfolds within the heart—where devotion to the Blessed Virgin Mary transforms into an enduring covenant. Pierced by the luminous simplicity of a Mother's love, souls discover a deeper purpose, moving from mere admiration to an abiding consecration. Here, the sacred embraces the mundane as Mary's virtues become living beacons, guiding one's path through daily trials and triumphs. Each act of piety, each whispered prayer, weaves a tapestry of divine love, resilient against the world's ephemeral promises. Thus, conversion is not an endpoint but a continual ascent towards heaven, ever accompanied by the gentle, unwavering hand of Our Lady, leading us closer to Christ through her immaculate embrace.

Personal Testimonies

From the bustling streets of Rome to the quiet corners of small villages, the transformative touch of Our Blessed Mother has left an indelible mark on countless souls. These personal testimonies converge into a grand symphony, each note resonating with the profound love and unwavering commitment to the Virgin Mary. They are not mere anecdotes but sacred narratives, echoing the whispers of a mother's plea and the resounding embrace of her grace.

One evening, in a candlelit church hidden among the rolling hills of Tuscany, Father Dominico stood at the altar, his heart heavy with doubts and burdens. His many years in the priesthood had been filled with service, yet he felt a yearning, an emptiness that neither duty nor sacrament could fill. It was then, beneath the serene gaze of a statue of Our Lady, that he experienced a moment of profound clarity. As he whispered a simple prayer, "Mother, guide my weary soul," an overwhelming sense of peace washed over him, enveloping him in a warm, maternal embrace. It was as if Mary herself stood beside him, softening his heart and enlightening his path. Father Dominico's life was forever changed; he became a fervent advocate of Marian devotion, encouraging others to find solace in her loving arms.

Then there is Isabella, a young woman from a bustling city in Spain, whose testimony speaks of quiet miracles. Caught in the throes of modern life, Isabella found herself drifting away from her faith. She stumbled one day upon a small Marian shrine tucked away in a hidden alley. Captivated by the simple beauty of the place, she knelt before Our Lady and began to weep, releasing years of pain and confusion. It wasn't an apparition or a spectacular vision that moved her, but a gentle, almost imperceptible shift in her heart – a reassurance that she was not alone. That moment marked the beginning of her return to the Church, where she found her vocation in serving the needy with unwavering devotion, guided always by the compassionate hand of Mary.

Such testimonies are not limited to the laity or clergy alone. In bustling convents, where the silence is only broken by prayer, nuns like Sister Maria of the Holy Rosary recount stories of small but profound Marian experiences. She recollects the night she lay awake, burdened with the fears of an impending decision. In the stillness, she began to pray the Rosary, each "Hail Mary" a step toward clarity. As dawn broke, she felt a serene conviction – Mother Mary had gently guided her to a resolution. These small, almost imperceptible encounters ripple through the lives they touch, weaving a tapestry of faith strengthened through Marian intercession.

Father Alejandro, serving in a rugged parish high in the Andes, shares a story intertwined with the trials of his community. Isolated and often forgotten, the villagers struggled with despair and poverty. One night, after leading the Rosary, Father Alejandro dreamt of Mary, clothed in radiant light, extending a mantle over the entire village. Awaking with renewed hope, he inspired his community to build a chapel dedicated to Our Lady. The villagers worked tirelessly, and as the chapel's foundation was laid, so too were the foundations of renewed faith and hope. Miraculous changes followed: bountiful harvests, improved health, and, most importantly, a rekindled spiritual unity. The villagers claim that it was Mary's intercession that turned their plight into a testament of faith.

These stories echo across the centuries, from the earliest converts of Christianity to modern-day believers. Consider, for a moment, the life of Blessed Carlo Acutis, a young Italian boy who found a profound connection to Mary even amidst his battle with leukemia. In his short yet impactful life, Carlo viewed the Rosary as a "ladder to Heaven," climbing it daily with the fervor of a mystic. His devotion to Mary was not born from miraculous visions but from a simple, profound trust in her ability to lead him closer to Jesus. Even in his final days, Carlo's unwavering faith and Marian devotion inspired countless others, proving that the flame of Mary's love burns brightly across generations.

Yet, it's not solely the famous or the clergy who carry these testimonies. Everyday believers, like Matteo, a fisherman from Sicily, find solace in the Rosary's rhythm amid the vast, unpredictable sea. Matteo recalls a storm so fierce it threatened to swallow his boat whole. Gripping his Rosary, he cried out to Mary, surrendering his fear and putting his life in her hands. The storm calmed, not instantly but gradually, as if Mary herself was guiding his boat to safer waters. Matteo's faith was not just renewed; it became an anchor, a testament to Mary's protection and the power of prayer.

In these testimonies, one perceives a common thread of tangible encounters with the intangible, divine intervention in the guise of maternal care. They underscore a profound truth: Mary's presence is felt not through grandiose miracles alone but in the quiet, personal shifts of the heart. Indeed, the magnitude of her love isn't quantified by the spectacular but by the deeply personal, transformative experiences that draw souls closer to Christ.

Consider also the story of Lucia, a teacher in Brazil, who begins each school day early with a silent prayer before a small statue of Our Lady in her classroom. Her dedication to Mary brings a calming order to her often chaotic day. When a troubled student joins her class, Lucia prays specifically to Mary for guidance. Over time, she witnesses a noticeable change in the child's behavior, a blossoming self-esteem and academic improvement that she attributes to Mary's intercession. The subtle presence of Mary in her daily routine had not only transformed her spirit but also touched the lives of her students.

Journeying into the heart of Africa, one finds the story of Father Emmanuel, a missionary in a remote village. Amidst the strife and challenges of his mission, it is a simple, tattered image of Our Lady that becomes his beacon. Father Emmanuel's dedication to Marian devotion leads to a revival of faith in his village. The people, once distant from the Church, now gather eagerly to pray the Rosary. Father Emmanuel attributes this spiritual transformation to the tender, often silent intercession of Mary, who, with a mother's love, gathers her children back into the fold.

Finally, consider the life of Anna, a new convert from a small American town who discovered her love for Mary through a seemingly coincidental moment. Browsing through her grandmother's attic, she found a dusty, old Marian prayer book. Intrigued, she began to read and recite the prayers. What started as a casual interest soon kindled into a blazing devotion. Anna's newfound faith deepened her relationship with Christ and animated her daily life with a sense of purpose and peace she had never known.

These personal testimonies, rich and varied, underline the quiet yet powerful presence of Our Lady in the lives of the faithful.

They remind us that devotion to Mary is not a relic of the past but a living, breathing testament to her enduring influence. Through these

Steps Toward Devotion

In the hush of a twilight prayer, where the evening sky melds with the deep azure of night, begins the journey of devotion. It's not a sudden transformation but a series of steps, each imbued with sacred significance, that lead a soul toward a fervent dedication to the Blessed Virgin Mary. These steps, like the subtle brushstrokes on a master artist's canvas, shape the contours of one's spiritual life.

First, there is the recognition. A soul in its restless wanderings finds a serene harbor in Mary's maternal love. This recognition is no mere intellectual consent but an inner realization, a moment of clarity when the heart acknowledges the radiance of Mary's virtues. The purity, humility, and mercy that emanate from her stand as a beacon of light, guiding the soul through life's tumultuous seas. Staring into the visage of the Madonna, one sees not just a mother, but the epitome of divine grace.

The next step is the embrace of Mary's virtues. Herein lies the heart of the matter—to embody the virtues exemplified by the Blessed Virgin. Purity, prudence, humility, and faithfulness become the guiding principles of life. This is not an imitation born out of mechanical repetition but a transformative engagement of the will. To seek Mary's purity is to recognize the value of chastity in thought and deed. To embrace her humility is to eschew pride, even in the smallest of things. Patience and mercy become one's daily bread, ensuring that in all interactions, grace prevails.

Contemplation forms the next step, a silent yet powerful phase in the journey. In the quiet stillness of prayer and meditation, the soul lies open to divine whispers. The rosary, with its rhythm of prayer and meditation, forms the soul's language of love to the Virgin. Each bead becomes a stepping stone toward deeper intimacy with Mary. The Angelus, recited humbly at dawn, noon, and dusk, transforms the ordinary flow of time into sacred intervals, moments where the soul reconnects with the mysteries of the Annunciation and Incarnation. These moments of contemplation draw the soul closer to the sacred heartbeat of Mary.

Engagement with the Sacred Scriptures follows naturally as the next step. Mary's presence in the sacred texts of both the Old and New Testament offers a rich tapestry for reflection. To see her foreshadowed in the Old Testament, an ark of a new covenant, and fulfilled in the New Testament as the Mother of God incarnate, enriches the soul with profound insights. The Magnificat, her song of praise, becomes the soul's anthem, echoing through the corridors of faith.

The step of Sacred Tradition involves immersing oneself in the steadfast teachings of the Church about Mary. Early Church Fathers, with their reverence and theological acumen, provide fertile ground for understanding Mary's role as Theotokos. Through the ages, saints and theologians have painted glorious pictures of Marian devotion. Their writings and reflections act as spiritual compasses, guiding the soul toward a mature and steadfast commitment to Mary.

Then there is participation in the Holy Sacraments, especially the Eucharist, which becomes a profound method to unite with Jesus and, by extension, with His Blessed Mother. During the Holy Communion, one senses Mary's presence, as if she's gently guiding one to her Son. This step is marked by an increased reverence and an awareness of Mary's maternal touch in the sacramental life of the Church. The sacraments, seen through Mary's eyes, become avenues of grace, channels through which divine love flows freely.

Personal testimony and communal celebration form another vital step. Witnessing to Mary's role in one's life, sharing moments of divine intervention, and celebrating Marian feasts such as the Assumption, the Immaculate Conception, and Our Lady of Sorrows, invite a communal acknowledgment of Mary's grace. Standing shoulder to shoulder with fellow devotees, the individual soul finds strength in community, comforted by the shared experience of Marian love. Hymns and prayers sung in unison become a symphony of devotion, ascending as a fragrant offering to the heavens.

Finally, the soul reaches the step of total consecration. This is the pinnacle, where one places oneself wholly under Mary's maternal care. It's an act of trust, surrendering one's life with its joys, pains, hopes, and fears into her hands. The act of consecration, often formalized through a special prayer or ceremony, symbolizes the soul's firm commitment to follow Mary's example. Through this total consecration, the soul enters into a deeper relationship with Mary, who leads it ever closer to her Son, Jesus Christ.

Thus, the journey of devotion is marked by steps both simple and profound, each drawing the soul ever deeper into the mystery of divine love as embodied by the Blessed Virgin Mary. It is a journey that transcends mere habit and touches the realms of the sacred, drawing the faithful into a dance of grace, led by Mary, the Mother of all.

Conclusion

In the resplendent tapestry of Divine Providence, the Blessed Virgin Mary shines with an unparalleled brilliance, illuminating the pathways of faith and guiding countless souls toward her Son, our Lord Jesus Christ. Indeed, Mary stands as the ever-radiant Star of the Sea, beckoning us with her tender gaze and maternal solace. Her example of love and virtue urges us to transcend the confines of our worldly existence and aspire to the heavenly ideals she embodies.

Through the chapters we've delved into, we've examined the profound significance of Marian dogmas, each a testament to Mary's unique role in the salvific history. Her immaculate conception, perpetual virginity, assumption, and other titles bequeathed by the Church attest to the divine artistry that fashioned her. Thus, she is not just a distant heavenly figure but an intimate intercessor, a mother who understands and responds to the pressing needs of her children on Earth.

Reflecting on the virtues of Mary presents a call to imitate her purity, humility, and unwavering faithfulness. These virtues are not mere abstract ideals but lived realities that we can strive to incorporate into our daily lives. Mary's life exemplifies how a soul intricately woven with grace can transform ordinary moments into divine encounters, revealing how earthly limitations can be transcended through heavenly grace.

The sacred texts paint a rich and evocative portrait of Mary, from the ancient prophecies of the Old Testament to the New Testament's fulfillment. This depiction binds her story intricately with the story of salvation, showing us that Mary's fiat, her "yes," was not just a moment in time but an eternal echo that continues to resound within the fabric of salvation history. Through Scripture, we discern how Mary's life is in constant dialogue with the divine will, a dance of obedience and love that brings forth the light of Christ into the world.

Mary's enduring presence throughout Sacred Tradition, revered by early Church Fathers and celebrated through the ages, speaks volumes about her perennial relevance. Saints and theologians have lavished upon her praises and titles, each an attempt to encapsulate her boundless grace and virtue. Their veneration assures us that the devotion to Mary is not a relic of the past but a living tradition continually enriched by the faith of generations.

Theological and philosophical reflections on Mary further enrich our understanding, offering deeper insights into her role and virtues. The Church's Mariology doesn't merely speak to her physical motherhood but her spiritual maternity over all creation. Philosophical contemplations on her virtues of wisdom and fortitude invite us to consider how these attributes can fortify our own spiritual journeys, guiding us to a more profound relationship with the Divine.

The scientific perspectives, too, offer intriguing insights, particularly the miracles attributed to Mary and the mysterious connections with the Shroud of Turin. Such reflections invite us to see that the intersection of faith and reason, far from being antagonistic, actually illuminates the fuller picture of Mary's impact on our world and on individual souls.

Homilies on Marian feasts, hymns sung in her honor, and prayers recited with fervor, all converge to exalt Mary and underscore her pivotal role in guiding the faithful. The liturgical celebrations and heartfelt devotions reveal the depth of love and reverence the Church holds for her. These sacred traditions and expressions of faith are not mere formalities but are imbued with spiritual vitality and transformative power.

Marian dogmas have faced objections and criticisms, yet, through careful defense and elucidation, the integrity and necessity of these beliefs are upheld. Scriptural and historical evidence corroborates the Church's teachings, fortifying the faithful's devotion and understanding. It is through this robust defense that the beauty and truth of Marian doctrines stand resilient against doubt and skepticism.

Personal testimonies of conversion and commitment underscore the transformative power of Mary's intercession. These stories resonate with the profound impact of encountering Mary — from moments of despair metamorphosed into hope to lives redirected toward divine service. Their narratives become a mosaic of faith, each piece contributing to the larger masterpiece of Marian devotion.

In concluding this exploration, it is evident that the Blessed Virgin Mary occupies a singularly unique and exalted place within the Christian spiritual landscape. Her life and virtues call us to a higher aspiration, inviting a deeper conversion of heart and mind. As we meditate upon her role and influence, let us allow her motherly guidance to permeate our lives, drawing us closer to the ultimate source of all grace, her Son, Jesus Christ.

May the Virgin Mary, Mediatrix of all graces and the embodiment of divine love and perfect obedience, continue to inspire and intercede for us. Let us commit ourselves to greater devotion, invoking her aid in all our endeavors, confident in her powerful and loving intercession. As we forge ahead in our spiritual journey, let the presence of Mary be our comfort and guide, leading us ever closer to the heart of God.

In her, we find a perfect model of holiness, an unerring guide to the Christian life, and an unwavering intercessor. Through her, we are drawn into the mystery of God's love, forever unfolding and inviting us deeper into divine communion. Thus, as we conclude, we do not part ways with our contemplation of Mary but, instead, invite her ever more deeply into our lives, letting her form our hearts anew in the fire of divine love.

Appendix A: Appendix

In the sacred continuum of divine revelations and the unwavering devotion to the Blessed Virgin Mary, this appendix serves as a wellspring for further exploration and deepening of one's faith. Here, we provide a curated selection of readings, prayers, and resources to guide you on your spiritual journey towards a more profound veneration of Our Lady.

Recommended Marian Readings

The treasure trove of writings dedicated to the Blessed Virgin Mary offers insights into her virtues, her role in salvation history, and the marvels attributed to her intercession. We recommend delving into the following texts to nourish your soul and enrich your understanding:

1. **"True Devotion to Mary"** by St. Louis de Montfort

2. **"The Glories of Mary"** by St. Alphonsus Liguori

3. **"Mary in the Middle Ages"** by Luigi Gambero

4. **"The World's First Love"** by Fulton J. Sheen

5. **"Mariology"** (Volumes I & II) edited by Juniper B. Carol, O.F.M.

Prayers and Devotions

Throughout the ages, the faithful have turned to Mary in prayer, seeking her intercession and meditating upon her life and virtues. Here are some traditional and powerful devotions to incorporate into your daily life:

- **The Rosary** – A contemplative prayer reflecting on the mysteries of Christ's life through Mary's eyes.

- **The Angelus** – Recited thrice daily to honor the Incarnation.

- **Litany of Loreto** – A series of invocations praising Mary's sublime qualities and asking for her protection.

- **Marian Novenas** – Nine days of prayer for special intentions through Mary's intercession.

- **Memorare** – A short, fervent plea for Mary's help based on her unfailing intercession.

Contact Information for Marian Societies and Organizations

For those seeking to deepen their devotion within a community, numerous societies and organizations are dedicated to honoring the Blessed Virgin Mary. They offer spiritual support, educational resources, and opportunities for communal prayer and service.

- **The Legion of Mary** – *Email:* contact@legionofmary.org

- **The Militia Immaculatae** – *Email:* info@militia-immaculatae.org

- **Family of Mary** – *Email:* office@familyofmary.org

- **Association of Mary, Queen of All Hearts** – *Email:* queenhearts@maryqueen.org

- **Marian Fathers of the Immaculate Conception** – *Email:* inquiries@marian.org

May this appendix serve not merely as a conclusion, but as an invitation to a lifelong pilgrimage alongside our Blessed Mother. Each step you take in devotion not only glorifies Mary but brings you closer to the heart of her Son, our Lord, Jesus Christ.

Recommended Marian Readings

The immense and boundless beauty of Marian devotion is illuminated through the works of many venerable authors and saints. Each bears witness to the mysteries and graces bestowed by the Blessed Virgin Mary. Through their words, the ineffable love and virtues of Our Lady are brought to light, inviting every reader to a deeper communion with her and, consequently, with her divine Son.

For those seeking to intensify their love and understanding of the Mother of God, the *Glories of Mary* by Saint Alphonsus de Liguori is indispensable. This classic, filled with soulful reflections and prayers, contemplates the magnificent attributes and intercessory power of Mary. Saint Alphonsus' poetic language and theological insights create a symphony of reverence, guiding the soul toward a profound appreciation of Marian devotion.

In his monumental work, *True Devotion to Mary*, Saint Louis de Montfort unveils the path to sanctity through consecration to Jesus through Mary. This spiritual masterpiece offers a structured approach to Marian consecration, emphasizing the transformative power of total dedication to the Blessed Virgin. Montfort's theological rigor coupled with his profound spiritual insight makes this treatise essential reading for anyone serious about Marian spirituality.

For a scholarly yet deeply moving examination, one ought to delve into *Mary in the Mystery of the Covenant* by Pope Saint John Paul II. This work eloquently articulates the role of Mary within the context of God's salvific plan. It resonates with the profound philosophical underpinnings and mystical understanding that marked John Paul II's papacy, presenting Mary as the bridge between the Old and New Covenants.

No Marian library would be complete without *The Complete Virgin Mary* by Michael O'Brien. Through narratives and reflections, O'Brien portrays the Blessed Virgin with an artist's eye and a mystic's heart. His writing paints vivid pictures, bringing to life Mary's role in both historical and transcendent dimensions.

For those intrigued by the intersection of Mariology and ecclesiology, *Hail, Holy Queen: The Mother of God in the Word of God* by Scott Hahn offers an accessible yet theologically rich exploration. Hahn's scriptural exegesis and theological reflections draw from Patristic insights and contemporary scholarship, presenting Mary not only as the Mother of Jesus but also as the Mother of the Church.

Another contemporary gem is *The World's First Love: Mary, the Mother of God* by Fulton J. Sheen. Sheen's eloquent prose and spiritual depth craft a compelling narrative that is as personable as it is profound. His meditations reveal the heart of Mary's virtues and her integral role in God's plan of redemption.

Saint Thomas Aquinas wrote comparatively little directly on Marian themes, but his treatment in *The Summa Theologica* on the privileges of the Blessed Virgin remains foundational. Aquinas's precise and logical approach provides robust theological foundations that support the Marian dogmas of the Church.

For a poetic and mystical approach, Dante Alighieri's *Divine Comedy* especially in *Paradiso*, channels Marian devotion through exquisite verse. Mary's presence as Mediatrix and Queen adorns the poet's theological journey, symbolizing the soul's ascent toward divine communion.

To understand Mary's role in modern devotion, one should consider *Redemptoris Mater*, the encyclical by Pope Saint John Paul II. This document outlines not just the doctrinal truths but also the pastoral applications of Marian devotion, emphasizing her role as Mediatrix and Advocate.

For those seeking the early roots of Marian devotion, the *Homilies on the Mother of God* by Saint Gregory of Nyssa and the writings of Saint John Damascene offer invaluable insights. These early

Church Fathers illuminate how the earliest Christian communities venerated Mary, fostering an appreciation for the historical continuity of Marian doctrine.

Bishop Fulton's Sheen's *Mary, Mother of All* is yet another marvelous contribution. This well-loved work envelops readers in profound reflections, making Mary's virtues and her role in salvation history a vivid reality for all who read it.

Perhaps one might also consider *Mary, Handmaid of the Lord* by Saint Teresa of Ávila. Though not exclusively focused on Mary, Teresa's writings offer glimpses into how Marian devotion infused her contemplative life, providing a mystical approach to understanding Mary's influence on the soul's interior journey.

Finally, *The Life of the Blessed Virgin Mary* by Anne Catherine Emmerich, based on her mystical visions, offers a deeply personal and unique portrayal of Mary's life that captivates both the heart and the mind. While not a theological treatise, Emmerich's poetic narrative enriches the reader's appreciation for the lived experiences and hidden joys of Mary.

Each of these recommendations invites deeper contemplation, greater devotion, and a fuller integration of Mary's virtues into the fabric of daily life. Through these writings, may our hearts be ever more enkindled with love for the Blessed Virgin, leading us closer to her Son, Our Lord Jesus Christ.

Prayers and Devotions

The divine tapestry of Roman Catholic tradition is rich with the threads of prayers and devotions dedicated to the Blessed Virgin Mary. These practices, infused with centuries of faith, are not mere rituals but profound expressions of love and reverence. They serve as spiritual bridges, connecting us to the maternal heart of Mary and, through her, to her Son, Jesus Christ. Let us embark on a journey through these sacred devotions, exploring their significance and their ability to transform hearts and minds.

The Rosary, often referred to as the Rose Garden of Mary, is a prayerful meditation on the mysteries of Christ's life through the eyes of His Blessed Mother. With each decade, we delve into the Joyful, Sorrowful, Glorious, and Luminous Mysteries, contemplating the pivotal moments in salvation history. The rhythmic repetition of the Hail Mary is not mere recitation but an offering of roses, each one a fragrant bloom in the garden of our soul. It weaves a tapestry of grace, as each bead passes through our fingers, inviting us to experience the divine presence.

In the Angelus, we commemorate the Annunciation, the sublime moment when the Word became flesh. This devotion, traditionally recited thrice daily, is a call to pause and reflect on the mystery of the Incarnation. As the Angelus bell tolls, it invites the faithful to embrace a moment of profound silence and contemplation. This prayer is a humble acknowledgment of our dependence on God's grace, and an invitation for Mary to guide us in our daily lives.

More often than not, the Litanies and Novenas to Mary become a wellspring of spiritual strength. These prayers, whether public or private, are solemn invocations, seeking Mary's intercession in various needs and situations. The Litany of Loreto, with its poetic cadence and rich titles, such as Mother of Divine Grace and Mystical Rose, encapsulates the many facets of Mary's role in our salvation. Novenas, on the other hand, are a nine-day journey of deep prayer, often preceding Marian feasts or seeking a special grace. They mirror the nine months she carried Jesus within her womb, a period of anticipation and trust in God's providence.

The Scapular of Our Lady of Mount Carmel is a symbol of Mary's protective mantle. This small garment, worn with faith and devotion, serves as a reminder of her constant care and intercession. It's a pledge of salvation, echoing the promise of Mary to Saint Simon Stock that those who die wearing the scapular shall not suffer eternal fire. This simple act of wearing the scapular grows into a profound commitment, aligning one's life with Marian virtues and seeking sanctity under her guidance.

In Marian consecrations, we devote ourselves entirely to Mary, entrusting our lives, hopes, and sorrows into her loving hands.

Saint Louis de Montfort's "Total Consecration" is a rigorous spiritual exercise, leading to a complete renunciation of self and a wholehearted surrender to Mary. Through this devotion, we ask Mary to assist in purifying us, to lead us to an intimate union with Jesus. It is a pathway of transformation, where one's heart beats in rhythm with the Immaculate Heart of Mary.

The Stations of the Cross, seen through Mary's perspective, provide a profound meditation on the Passion of Christ. This devotion, sometimes known as the Way of the Cross with Mary, allows the faithful to accompany Jesus in His suffering, through the sorrowful heart of His mother. Each station becomes a prayer of solidarity, a walk beside Mary, witnessing her strength and sorrow. It's an invitation to enter into the depth of Christ's love and Mary's untiring faith.

The Chaplet of the Seven Sorrows invites us to dwell on the significant moments of Mary's suffering, from the prophecy of Simeon to the burial of Jesus. This devotion opens our hearts to the profound sorrow Mary endured, pointing us toward the redemptive value of suffering when embraced with faith. Each bead of this chaplet is a tear, shed in union with the Mother of Sorrows, contemplating the mystery of suffering and its role in God's salvific plan.

In addition, the Exquisite simplicity of the Memorare prayer embodies the essence of Marian devotion, a powerful plea for her intercession. The words "Remember, O most gracious Virgin Mary" echo through the hearts of those in need, inviting Mary's tender compassion into moments of anguish and despair. Countless testimonies from the faithful recount the miraculous interventions attributed to this heartfelt invocation.

Moreover, various local and cultural Marian devotions infuse the broader tapestry with more vibrant threads. For instance, the Posadas in Latin America re-enact the Holy Family's search for shelter in Bethlehem, blending communal prayer and festive tradition. Each of these cultural practices reflects the universal appeal of Mary, a mother who transcends boundaries and speaks to the hearts of her diverse children.

In a quieter, personal space, the contemplation of Marian icons and images offers another avenue for devotion. Gazing upon the gentle yet strong visage of Our Lady of Perpetual Help or the serene countenance of the Black Madonna of Częstochowa, the faithful find solace and strength. These images are windows to the divine, inviting us to reflect on the mysteries of Mary's life and her continual presence in our lives.

Ultimately, each prayer and devotion directed to Mary is a step closer to a deeper union with Christ. They shape our spiritual landscape, infusing it with the fragrance of Mary's virtues. Through these practices, we invite Mary into our daily lives, asking her to intercede for us, to guide us, and to teach us to say "yes" to God's call with the same faith and humility she exhibited. As we traverse the various paths of Marian devotion, we find ourselves enveloped in her loving mantle, ever closer to the Sacred Heart of Jesus.

Contact Information for Marian Societies and Organizations

In the vast tapestry of devotion to the Blessed Virgin Mary, numerous societies and organizations stand as vibrant threads, interwoven with love and reverence. These groups act as spiritual beacons, illuminating the path towards a deeper connection with Our Lady, each with its unique charism and mission. They extend their hands to the faithful, inviting them to participate in this sacred journey, to drink from the well of Marian grace.

The heart of these organizations beats in rhythm with the profound mysteries of Mary's life and virtues. From local parish groups to international movements, they all share a common purpose: to exalt the Mother of God and propagate devotion to her. Connecting with these societies provides not just fellowship but also an opportunity for spiritual enrichment, education, and communal prayer.

Legion of Mary

Established in Dublin, Ireland, in 1921, the Legion of Mary has grown exponentially and now stretches across every continent. Members meet regularly to pray, engage in apostolic works, and deepen their Marian devotion. For further contact, interested individuals can visit their official website or connect with their local chapters found in many parishes worldwide. The central headquarters' contact information is as follows:

- Website: www.legionofmary.ie

- Address: Concilium Legionis Mariae, De Montfort House, Morning Star Avenue, Brunswick Street, Dublin 7, Ireland

- Email: *concilium@legion-of-mary.ie*

- Phone: +353 1 872 3153

In the shadows and light of modernity, *The Militia Immaculata* stands resolute as a beacon of Marian consecration. Founded by St. Maximilian Kolbe in 1917, this organization calls for a total consecration to the Immaculate Heart of Mary, encouraging the faithful to become instruments of Mary in winning souls for Christ. Their central team can be reached for more information:

- Website: www.consecration.com

- Address: *P.O. Box 5547, Peoria, IL 61601, USA*

- Email: *secretary@consecration.com*

- Phone: +1 331-223-5564

A soaring hymn in the symphony of Marian devotion sings from the Marianist Family. Enshrined in the charism of their founder, Blessed William Joseph Chaminade, the Marianists focus profoundly on Mary's role in the mission of Jesus. Their reach spans education, social justice, and parish life, and they offer pathways for deepening one's devotion to Mary through various forms of membership:

- Website: www.marianist.com

- Address: *Society of Mary, 4425 W. Pine Blvd., St. Louis, MO 63108-2301, USA*

- Email: *info@marianist.com*

- Phone: +1 314-533-1207

As a blossoming garden of piety, **The Marian Movement of Priests** nurtures sanctity among clergy and faithful alike. Founded by Father Stefano Gobbi, this movement thrives on cenacles of prayer, encouraging consecration to the Immaculate Heart and adherence to the messages allegedly given by Our Lady to Father Gobbi. Reach out for heart-to-heart contact:

- Website: www.mmp-usa.net

- Address: *P.O. Box 8, St. Francis, ME 04774, USA*

- Email: *info@mmp-usa.net*

- Phone: +1 207-398-3375

Radiating the light of Marian devotion, the *Daughters of Mary* seek to ignite the hearts of youth and families. Aiming to cultivate a deeper relationship with the Blessed Mother through various spiritual exercises, educational programs, and charitable works, the Daughters inspire a generational fidelity to Mary:

- Website: www.daughtersofmary.org

The eloquent whispers of the **Rosary Confraternity** echo through centuries, inviting the faithful to deepen their devotion to the Rosary. Stemming from the traditions of the Dominican Order, this Confraternity binds souls together in a global surge of prayer, elevating their supplications through the rhythm of the Hail Mary. For those seeking to weave their prayers into this celestial chorus, the following contact details open the door:

- Website: www.rosary-center.org

- Address: *Rosary Center, 543 Tyler Street, P.O. Box 3617, Portland, OR 97208, USA*

- Email: *rosary@rosary-center.org*

- Phone: +1 503-236-8393

Even as the sun sets, the brilliance of the Worldwide *Vanguard of Our Lady of Fatima* illuminates the globe, spreading the message of peace and conversion given by Our Lady to the shepherd children in Fatima. This organization, with its extensive network, is committed to fulfilling the requests of Mary through prayer, penance, and the dissemination of the Fatima message:

- Website: www.worldfatima.com

THE 15 PRAYERS OF ST. BRIDGET

 These Prayers and these Promises have been copied from a book printed in Toulouse in 1740 and published by the P. Adrien Parvilliers of the Company of Jesus, Apostolic Missionary of the Holy Land, with approbation, permission and recommendation to distribute them.
Pope Pius IX took cognisance of these Prayers with the prologue; he approved them May 31, 1862, recognising them as true and for the good of souls.

As St. Bridget for a long time wanted to know the number of blows Our Lord received during His Passion, He one day appeared to her and said: "I received 5480 blows on My Body. If you wish to honour them in some way, say 15 Our Fathers and 15 Hail Marys with the following Prayers (which He taught her) for a whole year. When the year is up, you will have honoured each one of My Wounds."

He made the following promises to anyone who recited these Prayers for a whole year:

1. I will deliver 15 souls of his lineage from Purgatory.

2. 15 souls of his lineage will be confirmed and preserved in grace.

3. 15 sinners of his lineage will be converted.

4. Whoever recites these Prayers will attain the first degree of perfection.

5. 15 days before his death I will give him My Precious Body in order that he may escape eternal starvation;

I will give him My Precious Blood to drink lest he thirst eternally.

6. 15 days before his death he will feel a deep contrition for all his sins and will have a perfect knowledge of them.

7. I will place before him the sign of My Victorious Cross for his help and defence against the attacks of his enemies.

8. Before his death I shall come with My Dearest Beloved Mother.

9. I shall graciously receive his soul, and will lead it into eternal joys.

10. And having led it there I shall give him a special draught from the fountain of My Deity, something I will not for those who have not recited My Prayers.

11. Let it be known that whoever may have been living in a state of mortal sin for 30 years, but who will recite devoutly, or have the intention to recite these Prayers, the Lord will forgive him all his sins.

12. I shall protect him from strong temptations.

13. I shall preserve and guard his 5 senses.

14. I shall preserve him from a sudden death.

15. His soul will be delivered from eternal death.

16. He will obtain all he asks for from God and the Blessed Virgin.

17. If he has lived all his life doing his own will and he is to die the next day, his life will be prolonged.

18. Every time one recites these Prayers he gains 100 days indulgence.

19. He is assured of being joined to the supreme Choir of Angels.

20. Whoever teaches these Prayers to another, will have continuous joy and merit which will endure eternally.

21. There where these Prayers are being said or will be said in the future God is present with His grace.

Each prayer is preceded by one Our Father and one Hail Mary.

Our Father, who art in heaven, hallowed be thy name.
Thy kingdom come.
Thy will be done on earth as it is in heaven.
Give us this day our daily bread and forgive us our
trespasses as we forgive those who trespass against us and
lead us not into temptation but deliver us from evil. **Amen**

Hail Mary, full of grace, the Lord is with thee; blessed art
thou among women and blessed is the fruit of thy womb,
Jesus.
Holy Mary, Mother of God, pray for us sinners, now and at
the hour of our death. **Amen.**

FIRST PRAYER
Our Father - Hail Mary.
O Jesus Christ! Eternal Sweetness to those who love Thee,
joy surpassing all joy and all desire, Salvation and Hope of
all sinners, Who hast proved that Thou hast no greater
desire than to be among men, even assuming human nature

at the fullness of time for the love of men, recall all the sufferings Thou hast endured from the instant of Thy conception, and especially during Thy Passion, as it was decreed and ordained from all eternity in the Divine plan.

Remember, O Lord, that during the Last Supper with Thy disciples, having washed their feet, Thou gavest them Thy Most Precious Body and Blood, and while at the same time thou didst sweetly console them, Thou didst foretell them Thy coming Passion.
Remember the sadness and bitterness which Thou didst experience in Thy Soul as Thou Thyself bore witness saying: "My Soul is sorrowful even unto death."

Remember all the fear, anguish and pain that Thou didst suffer in Thy delicate Body before the torment of the Crucifixion, when, after having prayed three times, bathed in a sweat of blood, Thou wast betrayed by Judas, Thy disciple, arrested by the people of a nation Thou hadst chosen and elevated, accused by false witnesses, unjustly judged by three judges during the flower of Thy youth and during the solemn Paschal season.

Remember that Thou wast despoiled of Thy garments and clothed in those of derision; that Thy Face and Eyes were veiled, that Thou wast buffeted, crowned with thorns, a reed placed in Thy Hands, that Thou was crushed with blows and overwhelmed with affronts and outrages.
In memory of all these pains and sufferings which Thou didst endure before Thy Passion on the Cross, grant me before my death true contrition, a sincere and entire confession, worthy satisfaction and the remission of all my sins. **Amen.**

SECOND PRAYER
Our Father - Hail Mary.
O Jesus! True liberty of angels, Paradise of delights, remember the horror and sadness which Thou didst endure

when Thy enemies, like furious lions, surrounded Thee, and by thousands of insults, spits, blows, lacerations and other unheard-of-cruelties, tormented Thee at will.

In consideration of these torments and insulting words, I beseech Thee, O my Saviour, to deliver me from all my enemies, visible and invisible, and to bring me, under Thy protection, to the perfection of eternal salvation. **Amen.**

THIRD PRAYER
Our Father – Hail Mary.
O Jesus! Creator of Heaven and earth Whom nothing can encompass or limit, Thou Who dost enfold and hold all under Thy Loving power, remember the very bitter pain.

Thou didst suffer when the Jews nailed Thy Sacred Hands and Feet to the Cross by blow after blow with big blunt nails, and not finding Thee in a pitiable enough state to satisfy their rage, they enlarged Thy Wounds, and added pain to pain, and with indescribable cruelty stretched Thy Body on the Cross, pulled Thee from all sides, thus dislocating Thy Limbs.

I beg of Thee, O Jesus, by the memory of this most Loving suffering of the Cross, to grant me the grace to fear Thee and to Love Thee. **Amen.**

FOURTH PRAYER
Our Father – Hail Mary.
O Jesus! Heavenly Physician, raised aloft on the Cross to heal our wounds with Thine, remember the bruises which Thou didst suffer and the weakness of all Thy Members which were distended to such a degree that never was there pain like unto Thine.

From the crown of Thy Head to the Soles of Thy Feet there

was not one spot on Thy Body that was not in torment, and yet, forgetting all Thy sufferings, Thou didst not cease to pray to Thy Heavenly Father for Thy enemies, saying: "Father forgive them for they know not what they do."

Through this great Mercy, and in memory of this suffering, grant that the remembrance of Thy Most Bitter Passion may effect in us a perfect contrition and the remission of all our sins. **Amen**.

FIFTH PRAYER
Our Father - Hail Mary.
O Jesus! Mirror of eternal splendour, remember the sadness which Thou experienced, when contemplating in the light of Thy Divinity the predestination of those who would be saved by the merits of Thy Sacred Passion.

Thou didst see at the same time, the great multitude of reprobates who would be damned for their sins, and Thou didst complain bitterly of those hopeless lost and unfortunate sinners.

Through this abyss of compassion and pity, and especially through the goodness which Thou displayed to the good thief when Thou saidst to him: "This day, thou shalt be with Me in Paradise." I beg of Thee, O Sweet Jesus, that at the hour of my death, Thou wilt show me mercy. **Amen**.

SIXTH PRAYER
Our Father - Hail Mary.
O Jesus! Beloved and most desirable King, remember the grief Thou didst suffer, when naked and like a common criminal.

Thou was fastened and raised on the Cross, when all Thy relatives and friends abandoned Thee, except Thy Beloved

Mother, who remained close to Thee during Thy agony and whom Thou didst entrust to Thy faithful disciple when Thou saidst to Mary: "Woman, behold thy son!" and to St. John: "Son, behold thy Mother!"

I beg of Thee O my Saviour, by the sword of sorrow which pierced the soul of Thy holy Mother, to have compassion on me in all my affliction and tribulations, both corporal and spiritual, and to assist me in all my trials, and especially at the hour of my death. **Amen**.

SEVENTH PRAYER
Our Father – Hail Mary.
O Jesus! Inexhaustible Fountain of compassion, Who by a profound gesture of Love, said from the Cross: "I thirst!" suffered from the thirst for the salvation of the human race.

I beg of Thee O my Saviour, to inflame in our hearts the desire to tend toward perfection in all our acts; and to extinguish in us the concupiscence of the flesh and the ardor of worldly desires. **Amen**.

EIGHTH PRAYER
Our Father – Hail Mary.
O Jesus! Sweetness of hearts, delight of the spirit, by the bitterness of the vinegar and gall which Thou didst taste on the Cross for Love of us, grant us the grace to receive worthily.

Thy Precious Body and Blood during our life and at the hour of our death, that they may serve as a remedy and consolation for our souls. **Amen.**

NINTH PRAYER
Our Father – Hail Mary.

O Jesus! Royal virtue, joy of the mind, recall the pain Thou didst endure when, plunged in an ocean of bitterness at the approach of death, insulted, outraged by the Jews.

Thou didst cry out in a loud voice that Thou was abandoned by Thy Father, saying: "My God, My God, why hast Thou forsaken me?"

Through this anguish, I beg of Thee, O my Saviour, not to abandon me in the terrors and pains of my death. **Amen.**

TENTH PRAYER
Our Father – Hail Mary.
O Jesus! Who art the beginning and end of all things, life and virtue, remembers that for our sakes Thou was plunged in an abyss of suffering from the soles of Thy Feet to the crown of Thy Head.

In consideration of the enormity of Thy Wounds, teach me to keep, through pure love, Thy Commandments, whose way is wide and easy for those who love Thee. **Amen.**

ELEVENTH PRAYER
Our Father – Hail Mary.
O Jesus! Deep abyss of mercy, I beg of Thee, in memory of Thy Wounds which penetrated to the very marrow of Thy Bones and to the depth of Thy being, to draw me, a miserable sinner, overwhelmed by my offenses, away from sin and to hide me from Thy Face justly irritated against me, hide me in Thy wounds, until Thy anger and just indignation shall have passed away. **Amen.**

TWELFTH PRAYER
Our Father – Hail Mary.
O Jesus! Mirror of Truth, symbol of unity, bond of charity,

remember the multitude of wounds with which Thou wast afflicted from head to foot, torn and reddened by the spilling of Thy adorable Blood. O great and universal pain, which Thou didst suffer in Thy virginal flesh for love of us! Sweetest Jesus! What is there that Thou couldst have done for us which Thou has not done!

May the fruit of Thy suffering be renewed in my soul by the faithful remembrance of Thy Passion, and may Thy love increase in my heart each day, until I see Thee in eternity: Thou Who art the treasure of every real good and every joy, which I beg Thee to grant me, O Sweetest Jesus, in heaven. **Amen.**

THIRTEENTH PRAYER
Our Father – Hail Mary.
O Jesus! Strong Lion, Immortal and Invincible King, remember the pain which Thou didst endure when all Thy strength, both moral and physical, was entirely exhausted, Thou didst bow Thy Head, saying: "It is consummated!"

Through this anguish and grief, I beg of Thee Lord Jesus, to have mercy on me at the hour of my death when my mind will be greatly troubled and my soul will be in anguish. **Amen.**

FOURTEENTH PRAYER
Our Father – Hail Mary.
O Jesus! Only Son of the Father, Splendour and Figure of His Substance, remember the simple and humble recommendation.

Thou didst make of Thy Soul to Thy Eternal Father, saying: "Father, into Thy Hands I commend My Spirit!" And with Thy Body all torn, and Thy Heart Broken, and the bowels of Thy Mercy open to redeem us, Thou didst Expire.

By this Precious Death, I beg of Thee O King of Saints, comfort me and help me to resist the devil, the flesh and the world, so that being dead to the world I may live for Thee alone.

I beg of Thee at the hour of my death to receive me, a pilgrim and an exile returning to Thee. **Amen.**

FIFTEENTH PRAYER
Our Father - Hail Mary.
O Jesus! True and fruitful Vine! Remember the abundant outpouring of Blood which Thou didst so generously shed from Thy Sacred Body as juice from grapes in a wine press.

From Thy Side, pierced with a lance by a soldier, blood and water issued forth until there was not left in Thy Body a single drop, and finally, like a bundle of myrrh lifted to the top of the Cross Thy delicate Flesh was destroyed, the very Substance of Thy Body withered, and the Marrow of Thy Bones dried up.

Through this bitter Passion and through the outpouring of Thy Precious Blood, I beg of Thee, O Sweet Jesus, to receive my soul when I am in my death agony. **Amen.**

CONCLUSION
O Sweet Jesus! Pierce my heart so that my tears of penitence and love will be my bread day and night; may I be converted entirely to Thee, may my heart be Thy perpetual habitation, may my conversation be pleasing to Thee, and may the end of my life be so praiseworthy that I may merit Heaven and there with Thy saints, praise Thee
forever. **Amen.**